NEW "SIMPLE" SOLUTIONS
TO LIFE'S LOVE PROBLEMS
AND
THE POLARITY OF MIND REFLEX

By

Dr. Daniel Materna Psy.D.

CONTENTS

CHAPTER SIX   57

The Importance of Conflict

CHAPTER SEVEN   63

Conflict Tools

Talk This Way to the Narcissist

In Summary

Ten Commandments for Caretakers

Ten Commandments for Highly Self-Preserving People

Fundamental Attachment Behaviors

Journaling As An Aid For Identifying Your Needs (And Meeting Your Next Best Friend)

DEDICATION

This book is dedicated to Julie.
Thank you for your love,
creativity, and encouragement.

INTRODUCTION

All people need secure and lasting love.

This book is about getting your needs met for secure and lasting love in life. If you have had repeated problems doing so, this is the book for you. But before we get started with describing a new way of understanding and solving love relationship problems, let's begin our discussion with two examples. Example #1 highlights the faulty and mutually destructive language people sometimes use in managing their conflicts. Example #2 offers a different and healthier style of language use, much more successful in creating secure feelings of love. Both examples include made-up characters with a make-believe problem. Pay close attention to the ways the different types of individuals use language to try and solve their conflict. I think the examples will be both instructive and emotionally moving for you. Please think about them both and what you like and don't like about them.

EXAMPLE #1:

Nate Narcissist: "What's wrong with you? Don't you know anything? I can't believe you even asked me such a stupid question! The dog is not sick."

Cathy Caretaker: "I'm sorry. I was only trying to help. He looks sick to me. Maybe he ate something bad. He's throwing up a lot…"

Nate Narcissist: "You've got to be kidding me? He's just a dog! You act like he's more important to you than I am.

Just put him outside for the night. He'll be better in the morning. Quit worrying so much about the damn dog!"

Cathy Caretaker: "OK. I'm sorry. I must be making too much about it. I'll let him out for the night.

Nate Narcissist: "Good. Let's go to bed."

(The next morning:)

Cathy Caretaker: "Oh my God! The dog is laying in the back yard and he's not moving! I think he's dead!"

Nate Narcissist: "You're overreacting. What's wrong with you anyway?"

(Cathy goes out to check on the dog. He died last night.)

Cathy Caretaker: "Oh my gosh, he's dead! The poor dog…. I knew we should have taken him to the vet! Why did I listen to you? How will I tell the kids?"

Nate Narcissist: "It's not the end of the world. Don't be such a baby! He's only a dog."

(Cathy walks away in tears. She feels mad at herself for listening to Nate and regrets it.)

To varying degrees, similar patterns of dominance, self-doubt, and invalidation of feelings and needs occur in many troubled marriages, friendships, and other types of relationships. We have to wonder, what is wrong with us as a species that we can engage in such aversive treatment between people who supposedly love each other? Now, let's review another example and compare it to the first one. (Again, the characters are made-up people as is their story of concern.)

EXAMPLE #2:

Mary Mutual: "You know I think the dog might be sick. He just threw up on the basement floor."

Mike Mutual: "What do you mean?"

Mary Mutual: "Come here and look."

Mike Mutual: "OK. Wow, you are right. Let's take him outside."

Mary Mutual: "I tried. He won't go. He doesn't want to be moved. I'm worried about him."

Mike Mutual: "Yes, so am I. What do you want to do?"

Mary Mutual: "Let's call the vet and take him in."

Mike Mutual: "But it's Sunday night?"

Mary Mutual: "We'll have to take him to the emergency clinic across town—it's open 24 hours."

Mike Mutual: "OK. Good idea. Let's lift him up together and get him into the car."

Mary Mutual: "OK. We can ask the neighbor to watch the kids, since they're sleeping."

Mike Mutual: "I'll call the neighbor. Can you pull the car out?"

Mary Mutual: "Ok. I hope he'll be all right."

Mike Mutual: "Me too."
(At the veterinarian's office treatment is quickly started to treat the dog for poisoning. The vet said he will survive and it was good that they didn't ignore how sick he was.)

Mary Mutual: "I'm so glad we didn't wait or minimize our concerns."

Mike Mutual: "Me too. I'm glad he'll be OK!"

In example #2 there were lots of shared concerns, good listening back-and-forth, and the expression of mutual ideas and needs. Mutual respect was evident between the partners. The love they shared was strengthened; their dog's problem and the way they handled it brought them closer rather than pushing them apart. (And, the dog survived!)

Now, with the two previous examples in mind, let's move forward and talk a little about our universal need for love. When we stop and think about it we all have a biological need for secure love, just like our other biological needs for healthy nutrition, clean air and pure water. Secure love is shown when one person demonstrates to another acts of valuing them consistently and over time. Interpersonal value is shown through acceptance, compassion, and the mutual respect of needs by one person to another. In fact, our need for safe and consistent love begins even before we are born. For example, how mothers live their lives while pregnant communicate to a child how loved they are. If the mother abuses alcohol or drugs or does not get good nutrition and sufficient rest, the baby's health can be negatively affected. Babies need health conscious mom's who are cautious with the substances and foods they ingest while pregnant. Similarly, how well the father treats the mother while she is carrying the child shapes the environment and context of love for the baby. If the father disregards the mother-to-be's needs for support and nurturance while pregnant, the additional stress the mother feels is also shared by the baby. Both parents play a part in insuring a secure and healthy environment while the baby is developing inside the mother.

Furthermore, parents need to continue supporting and loving each other, if they wish to foster secure circumstances in which their child will be raised. In the best of all worlds, love is fostered from conception and continues in healthy and secure ways thereafter.

However, life on Earth is not always secure or easy. Just like when our air or water gets polluted, we can become sick if the manner in which we receive love is compromised and unsecured. Our psychological, emotional, and physical well-being is not only at risk from conception, in regards to the nature of love we receive, but we are inherently vulnerable to problems caused by broken, abusive, or weakened love relationships our whole lives. That is, while toxins ingested during pregnancy and/or excessive family stress can have harmful effects on a fetus, we remain vulnerable to our environments and the nature of our love relationships until the day we die.

When our main love relationships are troubled, violated, compromised, or lost, be they with spouses, family, or friends, it can make us sick in a variety of ways. People can get depressed, lose sleep, and cope through maladaptive means when important relationships are going badly in their lives. Our emotional and physical health both suffer when love relationships go afoul. In extreme cases, some people may choose to give up their lives or even take the life of another after suffering a major love loss. Thus, secure and lasting love is vital to everyone's survival.

People generally realize that they must protect and maintain things of importance to them. For example, many people rely on automobiles to fulfill daily activities that serve to sustain them. We rely on our vehicles to get to work, take our kids to school, buy groceries, go on vacations, etc. Because we rely so heavily on them, most people put forth some effort to maintain their vehicles so that they are reliable and less likely to break down. Our cars get tune-ups, oil changes, inspections, alignments and the like. We realize we have to maintain them if we want them to last. Furthermore, they can be expensive to replace. But what about our love relationships? Don't they need similar attention and maintenance too?

How often do you hear of someone taking their love relationship in for maintenance? Most people only visit marital therapists and other counselors when their relationship is near total failure and break down is imminent. Being on the verge of divorce is typically the state of marriages that present for help and treatment. Marriage counseling is used as a last ditch effort for trying to avoid a total breakdown and failure of the relationship. But often little time and energy has been given to regular maintenance. People will too often "trade-in" their marriage or other significant relationship without learning about fixing what went wrong in the first place.

It's not just marital relationships that breakdown. We also rely on family, friends, coworkers, employers and our governments to meet various needs for life essential securities. But these relationships can break down too. Why is that? That is, if secure and lasting (love) relationships are crucial to our survival, what goes wrong so easily between people? And why don't we spend more time and effort fostering and maintaining the security of our relationships to best preserve our health and survival?

But, people are busy these days. We work, parent, shop, cook, clean, maintain homes, go to church, etc. It can be easy to conclude we have little time in today's world to invest in having more secure relationships. Once relationships go afoul, bringing love and healthy association back from the brink of disaster and failure is not easy. Sometimes it is impossible. Why is this?

A new perspective exists in the pages of this book. It is a perspective that puts forth a modern explanation for today's love (and other) relationship problems. I believe the ideas you'll learn about in this book help to explain the pervasive nature of our love troubles and, most importantly, what you can do about them. In addition, I have tried to write this book so that most people can benefit by it without having training and experience in the mental health profession. This does not mean mental health and other professionals will benefit less; indeed, the book sets forth a new theory about relationship problems and ways to resolve them that can benefit professionals and nonprofessionals alike. However, I have tried to make the book informative and entertaining by referencing various movies and songs familiar to many people. I have not emphasized the mental health theories that have also served as the formative basis for the ideas presented here. The latter would be a different type of book for a different audience. But it is appropriate to assume the ideas in this book have a sound theoretical basis and represent an integration of a wide body of mental health knowledge and clinical experience.

In this book, I introduce an idea about how our brain's fight-or-flight response, the protective and integrated emotion based system found in the "wiring" of our brain, may actually <u>interfere</u> with secure love and lasting attachments with others. I refer to this process as the "Polarity of Mind Reflex." The "Polarity of Mind Reflex" may best be defined in reference to how our brains guide us towards two different types of actions whenever we are in danger. The "danger" in regards to this book is the fear and anxiety our brains automatically experience whenever our primary love interests are threatened for any number of reasons. That is, our fight-or-flight response system directs us towards two types of behaviors that determine how we structure our love relationships. One way is through seeking love by placing more demands and needs on others (fight response). The other way is somewhat paradoxical because, in contrast to the first way, we also tend to sacrifice our needs for the needs of others (flight response) in hope they will value and love us more. Readers might be familiar with other descriptive terms characterizing extremes in the first (fight) response such as selfish, self-centered, and narcissism. In contrast, people prone to responding excessively in the second response style (flight) have associated with them terms like caretaker, codependent, and victim. So it seems our brains might be working against us. Our fight-or-flight protective system may be complicating our attempts to establish the secure love we all desperately need.

In a way, although our fight-or-flight system use to be more heavily relied upon, for example when it was used to protect us from previous life threats like saber tooth tigers, now it may be working against our ability to establish secure love. Because secure and lasting love requires the <u>mutual</u> respect of both people's needs in relationships, but our fight-or-flight reflexes guide us against such mutual sharing by either directing us to either dominate or pacify each other in relationships, we are "wired" to fail in establishing lasting intimacies. That is, unless we learn ways to adapt and that is what this book is all about.

I wish to note to readers that the Polarity of Mind Reflex is a new idea. I have been a licensed clinical psychologist for 20 years and had a few more years working in the mental health field before that. As my work and studies progressed, and as they continue to do so, I realized there had to be a way of understanding, explaining, and changing our love relationship problems because they simply were repeating themselves for so many people. Since the Polarity of Mind Reflex is a new concept, no one should assume that it is a reflection of years of scientific research. Rather, it is a term and idea that simply "fits" the way our brains have historically been known to respond to threats and danger. Furthermore, the term has proven useful in reframing and, to a degree, normalizing common and pervasive relationship problems. The "Polarity of Mind Reflex" has proved to be a valuable concept in my work helping people understand why the ever-popular "selfish and caretaking" styles of relating fail in the goal of secure attachment with others. Someday, the Polarity of Mind Reflex may become a well-researched construct and an even more significant contribution to the field of mental health. But for now, remember that it is a new way of thinking about relationship problems and, more importantly, points towards alternative ways of modifying what have previously been intractable relationship issues. Later in Chapter 2 I will describe this theoretical Reflex in more detail.

This book also describes a theory for overcoming the limiting effects of the Polarity of Mind Reflex. In addition, it presents many tools and intervention strategies to counter the natural but negative effects the Reflex has on love and attachments with others. Such negative effects are seen in the way many relationship failures occur. Regardless of whether they occur in marriages, friendships, work-settings, or politics, <u>most relationship failures are due to the divide created in the struggle for whose needs will dominate the relationship at any given time</u>. The Polarity of Mind Reflex is a way of defining how our brain's fight-or-flight response may shape people in terms of needs fulfillment, but in an ineffective way when it comes to creating secure love.

Unfortunately, the fight-or-flight mechanism is better designed to counter physical threats, rather than the "threats" people experience in terms of intimacy and love. In addition, the fight-or-flight response is not automatically discriminating in terms of how it gets applied when people <u>feel</u> threatened in their relationship attachments. Thus, our brains engage in a battle for needs which get translated into words and actions in response to what is basic to our very survival. This battle is about whether our fundamental needs for secure love will be met in relationships and whose needs will dominate. Some of the typical terms for such relationship problems include patterns dominated by narcissism/selfishness and caretaking/codependency. As you read further in this book, you will see how the Polarity of Mind Reflex supports the creation of flawed relationship patterns and sabotages us in our attempts to achieve secure love. It is no wonder we have so much difficulty establishing and maintaining secure and lasting love. Our brains may be wired in such a way to defeat us, that is, unless we apply higher levels of thinking in negotiating and constructing relationships.

Once you read and understand the theory behind the Polarity of Mind Reflex, you will be better prepared to apply the skills and tools presented in this book. All the tools and advice are based on an over-arching goal of creating mutual respect in relationships. Mutual respect means that <u>both</u> individuals (and groups) express their needs <u>and</u> care about the needs of the other. The lack of mutual respect of needs in a relationship creates insecure and defective attachment leaving both parties vulnerable to loss and never-ending conflicts. Furthermore, when mutual respect is missing in relationships, people's fight-or-flight responses will dominate and relationships will become polarized and weaken over time. Thus, to avoid an endless tug-of-war of needs, mutual respect of needs is required to create trust between people and establish secure and lasting relationships or love.

It is also my opinion that the best ideas or theories about the causes of problems in life must lead to solutions and interventions that improve relationship functioning. People should feel good about seeing and experiencing signs of success as they work to shape relationships towards secure and lasting love. However, this does not mean that attempts to change are easy. In many cases it takes significant effort and perseverance to change non-mutual and polarized patterns of relating, especially when they have existed for many years.

You might be wondering why is it that "simple" solutions to relationship problems are easy to understand, logically anyway, but not always easy to apply? For example, most people have had the experience of seeing someone else headed for trouble in a relationship, but when given sound logical advice about it they continue on repeating the same behaviors that have caused them heartache before. Why is this? I think the reason is our brains. You see, much of our feelings are attended to by the right side of our brain while much of our logic is fabricated on the left side. Integration of both sides is necessary for healthy decision making in life, but this integration can be reduced when people are mistreated, abused, neglected or simply "misguided" in their childhoods. In these latter cases it appears as if our fight-or-flight responses—all automatic in our brains—dominate how we get our needs met in relationships. Thus, a fruitless tug-of-war of needs between people can be haphazardly created due to our brains responses to abusive or neglectful experiences early in life. This tug-of-war, if left unchanged, takes us farther away from the establishment of mutual respect of needs and the secure love it brings. Unfortunately, it is all too easy to fail in our quest for love.

Have you ever wondered why our childhoods are so darn important in terms of our mental health and relationship functioning? They are important because brain growth and the associated "wiring" of our brains are occurring in a fast and fundamental way early in life. Thus, our behavioral and relationship patterns are hard-wired into us during that time. Change thereafter, such as in adulthood, is harder and takes more practice and time to create it. Fortunately, our brains have "neuroplasticity" which means they can in fact change as adults. Also fortunate for us is that the way we communicate can alter the very circuitry of our brain. So you can teach an old dog a new trick! But practice and repetition is required, as is true for learning any new skill. This is especially true the older we get. (For helpful and informative discussions about our brains and how meditation/mindfulness can help increase the efficiency with which your brain can change see *Rewire Your Brain For Love,* by Dr. Marsha Lucas, 2012, and *Buddha's Brain,* by Drs. Rick Hanson and Richard Mendius, 2009. Also, see Appendix III in the back of this book to learn how to use journaling for similar purposes.)

But one of the things that make habit change so hard is the fact that as brains are being updated and changing, people typically experience feelings of anxiety and confusion. You might think that if we are on the right track in establishing new healthier patterns of achieving secure love, our brains and hearts would be jumping for joy? But why don't we, at first anyway? That is, why do we struggle to make wise and prudent changes in relationships that are more likely to enhance mutual respect and give us greater likelihoods of getting our needs met for secure love? I think it is because our fight-or-flight systems in our brains were formatted (wired) with a very different pattern earlier in life. (We will talk a lot about this in this book.) And, because our brain's main objective is our survival, it produces anxious feedback to us when we compel ourselves to act differently later in life. Thus, we must ride-out some uncomfortable feelings at first when we are changing habits that were vital to our survival in childhood but are defeating us as adults in terms of establishing secure intimacy with another person. It's a little like Darwin's theory of evolution. Our adaptions to relationship enhancement which are vital to our longevity and health only occur gradually overtime because our brains can only adapt at a gradual pace. Thus, try not to be too discouraged when associated feelings of anxiety and confusion arise as you learn to create mutual respect in your relationships. Such feelings can be considered necessary parts of the "brain change process." That is, you can think of your naturally occurring negative feelings and fears as a "gut-check" by your brain. Your brain just wants to be sure you know what you are doing in terms of updating your survival strategies and, in our case here, how you negotiate and achieve secure and lasting love.

Therefore, if the solutions and tools found in this book are going to be effective and worth your time and effort, then you yourself must persevere through your initial feelings of anxiety and confusion. Gradually you should start to feel and experience some growing sense of success and life enhancement, in terms of your own happiness, as you apply them. Similarly, the solutions and tools must result in positive signs of change in your relationships and/or be felt by you as improving your self-worth and growth. So pay attention to how you feel in your experiences to enhance relationships, as you apply the ideas and tools found in this book. Don't be discouraged by initial feelings of discomfort; being able to recognize even small positive signs of change can aid you in efforts to grow and move forward toward establishing healthier relationships and the love you seek.

And finally, one last note before proceeding. Unfortunately, there is no guarantee your current partner or another will work with you in the establishment of a more mutually respectful relationship. Therefore, by all means, please seek out the services of a licensed mental health professional to aid you in evaluating important relationship decisions before you make them. And regardless of whether you choose to stay in a relationship or not, the tools and ideas in this book can at least help you give your relationship another try. Furthermore, this book can give you the information needed to develop the skills required for establishing secure love, regardless of whether you get them met now or in the future.

Chapter 1

SOME THOUGHTS ABOUT LOVE

What did the Beatles and Jesus have in Common?

I have always been a big fan of the Beatles. Since my childhood in the 1960s, when the Beatles overtook the nation and much of modern day music, I have been easily captivated by their songs and lyrics. During that time, Beatles' music was heard on most radios, televisions, and home record players wherever you went. As their popularity grew, the Beatles were interviewed and frequently written about in magazines and newspapers. The evening news reported on them. Theatres showed their movies and they appeared on popular television shows like Ed Sullivan. Reaching television appearance status was remarkable at that time when you consider there were only three stations back then and no cable networks to appear on. But what made the Beatles' music so appealing to so many people? Looking back, the Beatles early music had one main message. Their songs heralded the essential nature love plays in our lives.

Yes, early on in their careers, the Beatles were all about finding and keeping love. Some of their songs and lyrics included: "All you need is love," "There's nothing you can do that can't be done with love," *She Loves You*, *Can't Buy Me Love*, and *Help (I Need Somebody)*. Their songs about love caught on like wild fire; people simply went crazy over them. "Love, love, love...." was what they were all about.

Looking back, the Beatles' first songs seemed to magically meet some universal need found in people's hearts, souls, and minds. One of its members, past-Beatle Paul McCartney, even went on to receive honorary knighthood from the Queen of England for his lifetime contributions. Clearly, the Beatles music was legendary and as song writers they contributed to the world in a way few others had. As Sir Paul and band Wings later sang in the 1970's there was, "Nothing silly about writing another silly love song." Like many others, I too appreciated the Beatles' contributions. We all eventually learn how vital love relationships are to our health and well-being. Whether it's through the normal experience of loss of a loved one or from repeated struggles with rejection and love failures, most people come to realize that, "Love isn't silly at all."

Ironically, even though the Beatles and their songs about love were welcomed by thousands of people, there was another side reacting to their popularity. In fact, the Beatles were not universally received with open arms. Surprisingly some people at that time were shocked and fearful about their popularity and ascribed a "danger" no reasonable person could foresee. Their music emblazoned love, but some people thought their music, and band, were a threat to the establishment existing in that era. Some even went to the extreme and considered the Beatles "devil-like" in nature. I never understood this as a kid grow-ing up. What could be so wrong with singing about love I wondered, especially with images of the Vietnam War glaring across the T.V. each evening? But now, following years of training and experience as a clinical psychologist and marital therapist, along with my own expe-riences in the "love losses" column of life, I think I understand the "threat" the Beatles represented. We are all vulnerable to the impor-tant role love plays in our lives.

Whenever something arises in our environment that imposes a risk of changing the nature and experience of love in our lives, we are sur-prisingly "in danger." That is, people don't do well when their primary love relationships are shaken-up by an outside source. Many people spend a lot of time structuring and controlling their love relationships, sometimes too much so. Some are even abusive to others in the pro-cess. People can go to great extremes to control the ways in which they receive love and maintain its steady supply in their lives. No wonder some reacted with suspicion and inflammatory accusations about the Beatles presence in the 1960s. It wasn't so much the message in their songs perhaps, but the fact that "Love relationships" were being conjured up in their lyrics and some people reacted fearfully when this happened. That is, some people react with fear and anxiety when their experience with Love is directly or indirectly stirred-up by an external force, even by something as harmless as a song.

For example, one person might be alarmed seeing their spouse or boyfriend/girlfriend talking to another of the opposite sex. Certainly more devastating insults occur to love relations through affairs and other types of infidelities. But to those who are most vulnerable in their attachments with others, even the extra attention given by others in social conversation, or song lyrics about the need for love, can trigger anxiety, insecurity, or threat. This isn't to overlook how the Beatles were also idolized for their looks and how others may have reacted jealously when their partners screamed hysterically at the mere sight of the Beatles. However, as is all too common, people frequently react to reminders about love relationship insecurities by projecting blame onto the "messenger." That is, harbingers of love can surprisingly be hated, looked upon suspiciously or vilified. It is kind of similar to Jesus' crucifixion; some people were threatened by his messages of love and look what happened to him!

The need for lasting love is vital to our survival. Generally speaking, we don't respond well to things that are viewed as threats to any of our basic needs. We are willing to go to war over such threats, as can be seen in the tensions residing in the Gulf zone of the Middle East. The oil must flow steadily or else our way of life may be seriously threatened. So it is with the flow of love; we don't always respond rationally to threats that could hamper its supply. And, as most people come to realize, the total loss of a primary love relationship can have devastating effects to one's way of life. People sometimes do crazy things when they fear their primary love relationship is threatened or when childhood vulnerabilities are later triggered in adult relationships. Like the rock singer Pink sings in her song *Please Don't Leave Me*, "Can't you tell that this is all just a contest, the one who wins will be the one who hits the hardest?" Many songs have been written about similar love battles. Some of the reasons for our vulnerabilities with love and their solutions will be covered in this book. Thus, if you have loved and lost, read on!

The importance of love in our lives has also been discussed and written about long before the Beatles sang and wrote of it. No doubt love has played an essential role in humans' lives since the beginning of mankind. Therefore, as I prepare to discuss new concepts essential to solving love relationship problems, I feel I also need to briefly highlight an important aspect of my own development. (Just to let you know some of what my brain was "absorbing" in my early years.) One of my earliest experiences with love came from what I was taught attending a Catholic grade school from first through eighth grades. It was the whole notion that God was love and Jesus was a sign of it. Similar to a lot of people, but certainly not everyone, Jesus' life was a symbol of God's love and was part of my earliest learning's about love. As I grew up in and around the Catholic Church, I learned that Jesus' symbolic life meant I was loved no matter what else happened to me. I gleaned a lot of comfort from this teaching, just like I did from Beatles' music. It is no coincidence that religions typically profess the universal principle of love, as it is a necessary and valued element in all our lives. My early life experience was just one example of it. So even though this is not meant to be a religious book, I thought my earliest teachings about love warranted some explanation including one other fundamental point I will discuss below.

In addition to Jesus' presence being a symbolic gesture of love, there was also emphasis placed on "The Golden Rule." The Golden Rule indicates we are all to: love your neighbor as you would your-self. Most importantly, the Golden Rule points out what each person needs to experience and express to others in order to create secure love in their lives. That is, people need to treat each other as they would like to be treated. Mutual respect for each other's needs is a key element in this book because it is <u>only</u> through the reciprocal creation of mutual respect between people that secure and lasting love can be established. This is true for Christians, Non-Christians, and Atheists alike; people have no chance of having secure and lasting love in their lives without mutual respect being woven into the fabric of their relationships.

However, for the sake of being very clear about the meaning of mutual respect as referred to in this book, mutual respect is not an excuse to project our needs onto others. That is, we need to understand how the other person wants to be treated (by asking them first) and not simply by guessing or treating them in terms of what we ourselves would want. In the latter case, our behaviors can grow dangerously close to acting in over-controlling and selfish ways. Each person needs to be in charge of how they prefer to have their needs met based on their own separate feelings. So in seeking the creation of mutual respect be sure to inquire what people need and don't assume things because you yourself like your needs met in certain ways. Thus, mutual respect and its relationship to secure love have to be worked at. But the value of it has been established since at least Jesus' time and it continues to be an essential part of healthy relating. In retrospect, just as, "Love, love, love," was sung by the Beatles, a similar tune was sent to humans from above. I believe this was more than just coincidence.

One Example of a Loving Person

Because this book is about establishing and maintaining secure love relationships, it seems only fitting that I describe someone from my life that was an expert at giving and sharing love and further influenced my thinking about it. The person I am referring to was my wife's Grandma Jones. When I met her as an adult, I watched how her relationships were marked by a great sense of love and compassion. She appeared to me to be doling out love like a baker bakes bread. I had never met anyone like her before. I did not know if she always lived her life in this way, but as a young adult she became my definition of "love personified." If Webster's Dictionary wanted to include a picture of someone who portrayed the meaning of love, it would be her's. She was able to touch and connect with me, in love, in a way I never knew existed. I marveled at how she made me and others feel. I thought about her a lot.

There were undoubtedly many sides to Grandma Jones. But, to describe Grandma Jones without referring to her spirituality would be unthinkable. Her spirituality was the primary ingredient of her life. From her religious beliefs she gained much strength and an extensive capacity for love. When you visited her, she could wrap you up in a feeling of being loved before you had a chance to take your coat off. Love was in the grip of her hugs. It was in the look of her eyes. It was in her kind and gentle spirit. It was in the way she listened, told stories, and showed compassion. She'd smile and laugh with you. If you teased her, she'd tease you back, but tell you if you went too far. She took pleasure in life. She enjoyed simple things like going for walks and sharing meals with people. She loved to cook and bake. She loved to eat. Yet, she stood tall, thin, and strong. The wall of her trailer was covered with saved greeting cards, tacked up and serving as symbols of relationships she shared. She gave a lot to others. In fact, she "adopted" more children and adults as her children and friends from her small town in the hills of Kentucky and from all the places she traveled to, than can ever be counted. She showed me and others the true power of love. Furthermore, love wasn't just a coating on her outside; it was in the yeast and flour of her soul. It was a great pleasure to be in her company. Should you have stopped and visited her in her hometown, doing so would have no doubt made your heart rise too. She may be gone now, but the nourishment found in her love remains. I speak for many. Perhaps you have known someone like her in your life? But, perhaps not. Whether or not you have please keep reading. Let's work on improving the chances of getting your love needs met.

Some Points About Love and War

The Beatles' music and its emphasis on love also came at a time when much of the world was stuck in another facet of the human condition: war. The aggression and turmoil associated with the Vietnam War likely inspired the message of love in the Beatles songs. Love certainly was needed. Similarly, the Bible describes many of the trials of the human condition such as aggression and death and spells out ways to cope with them. But what does all this mean when it comes to people's ability to follow the Golden Rule and practice mutual respect? When you consider how war and aggression are no strangers to the world we live in, what, therefore, makes it so difficult for people to apply mutual respect on a daily basis? It seems that a need exists to manage humans' propensity for aggression along with their parallel need for love. That is, a civilized world is basically a world that balances our need for love in relationships with our predisposition for aggression and self-protection. Human beings seem to be polarized around these two conflicting needs. On a daily basis, the polarization shows up in varying degrees of selfishness and caretaking behaviors within relationships. Thus these two seemingly opposite acts are automatically produced in our brain in an attempt to guarantee our survival. This can be seen in the majority of our relationships and the reciprocal nature of needs. People either (A) seek to dominate and have their needs met or, (B) coalesce and deemphasize their needs in hopes of avoiding rejection and abandonment. Thus, people typically fight for their needs and dictate the essence of their relationships or relinquish their needs and accept a caretaking role with others (The Polarity of Mind Reflex).

It can be argued that our happiness in life is really determined by the quality of the love we exchange with others. This idea is echoed in the song *The End* from the Beatles Abbey Road album. This song concludes, "And in the end, the love you take is equal to the love you make." In conjunction, acts of aggression and selfishness are "simply" indications that interpersonal routes toward exchanging love have become compromised and adversely affected by fear. When people are afraid to be hurt, they develop a need to pacify or dominate others. A few years before the Beatles were born, in 1933, Franklin D. Roosevelt was dead-on saying, "...all we have to fear is fear itself...." Likewise, in this book I'll discuss the ways fear interferes with secure love and what you can do about it.

When the world is at war, in some place or fashion, Love should automatically arise as a prominent aspect of our culture in books, songs, artwork, church and temple discussions, politics, etc. Together, love and war represent two ends of a spectrum. Love must intercede and redirect human's tendency towards aggression. In this way, the human condition can be seen as self-correcting and in the most basic of reframes, war can be viewed as "love gone badly." Thus, interpersonal domination of needs is at the heart of all wars and other major interpersonal conflicts. Somewhat similarly, the mutual respect of needs between warring parties is the only permanent path toward ending such conflicts.

In a related way, when a person has experienced significant rejection in childhood, the capacity to receive and give love in adulthood is often compromised. Fear and anxiety is typically felt reflexively in people who had maladaptive experiences with attachment growing up. Thus, the existence of fear in relationships indicates that something has gone wrong, or is going wrong, between two people in their exchange of love. Domestic violence, infidelity, jealousy, childhood abuse and abandonment are just a few signs of love gone badly. Totalitarian governments and despots are further examples that the dark side of human nature has metastasized, with "love" being captured and controlled through threats and aggression. War, in essence, might be seen as a last ditch effort to correct a person's or group's out of control efforts to contain the sources of love around them as seen in the heavy handed domination of others. Humans don't tend to improve over time without modifications to the ways love is exchanged with others. Help is needed. I foresee this book to be a piece of that help for the people who read it.

Love Has Its Limits

When a search is initiated on the internet for books about the need for love, several pop-up. However, if you also look up books with the words "love is <u>never</u> enough" you will find many of those too. Why is that? One example of books outlining the need for love is Bernie Siegel, M.D., who published books highlighting the essential nature of love and peace, especially in reference to bodily health. He emphasized the human need for love in physical healing and medicine. Conversely, psychologist Bruno Bettelheim wrote a book in 1950, *Love is Not Enough*, outlining the problems of indulging children with love. Basically, he wrote that kids have additional needs beyond "only" loving them that must be met. When parents adopt strictly a "feel good approach" when relating to their children and dole out love unconditionally, but without encouraging perseverance and effort (or mutual respect for others), they can mistakenly handicap their children. Additionally, Martin Seligman, Ph.D., wrote in *The Optimistic Child* that parents have to make requirements on kids and encourage their effort to learn coping skills for life. In this way children learn self-confidence and how to handle future problems. Thus, based on parenting philosophy and knowledge parents can instill "antidepressant skills" within their children. Parents do this by helping their kids develop coping skills and interpersonal habits that bypass excessive helplessness, dependency, and selfishness across the life span. As children learn to trust themselves and relate to others in mutually respectful ways, they also develop life skills that serve as antidotes to depression and low self-esteem. Therefore, love of a child is necessary, but not sufficient, in preparing them for life.

And in adult relationships, why isn't love for another enough to get the other person to return the love back to you? On a daily basis as a psychologist and marital therapist I am told stories of how people love others yet feel (or experience being) rejected and mistreated in return. Selfishness in one partner frequently trumps committed love in the other. Relationships often become out of balance and one-sided.

Overtime, people who restrict themselves to solely a caretaker's role grow tired, depressed, and depleted. Furthermore, as attention to the selfish partner decreases, which is inevitable, the selfish person experiences a struggle with the growing sense of not feeling loved so much anymore. Thus, even though the Bible advised otherwise as seen in Jesus' Golden Rule: "Thou shalt love thy neighbor as thyself. There is none other commandment greater than these." (*The Way The Living Bible Illustrated*, 1973, Mark 12:31), people repeatedly have problems doing so. Therefore, it seems neither loving others by itself nor the Golden Rule as commonly applied is sufficient in maintaining secure love relationships. Neither approach results in the reciprocal exchanges of love necessary for lasting attachment. The answer is not found in simply loving more in a unidirectional fashion. A need arises to explain, at least in a theory, why not. As stated in the Introduction our nervous system's fight-or-flight response (and Polarity of Mind Reflex) might be part of the reason. This book emphasizes the additional knowledge and skills necessary to achieve a healthy balance between caring for others' needs and asserting one's own needs.

On Towards Simple Solutions and Other Love Tools

The title of this book also highlights its intent toward defining "simple solutions" to life's love problems. By simple I mean solutions that are straight forward, logical, and easy to understand. Many of the solutions are based on the language people use when negotiating conflicts. But by no means are simple solutions always easy to apply, especially for people polarized in terms of caretaking or selfishness. Yet they are easy to understand and can be applied with success through perseverance and practice. In addition, if you believe that, "Love is the answer," as John Lennon sang in his song "Mind Games," and as God demonstrated by sending his only son to earth, then tools that support healthier love relationships are worth the time and effort they require.

Healthy love relationships are essential to being healthy individuals and creating a saner world.

The tools in this book can be applied immediately, but you will succeed more reliably if you understand the principles and theories behind them. People are more consistent in their efforts if they understand the reasons they are doing things. Furthermore, people will stick with the challenges required by such changes if they know what signs of progress to look for. For example, guaranteeing healthy relationships over time must be couched in other relationship sustaining skills. Such skills include not only mutual respect but knowing how to compromise, trust, and respect interpersonal boundaries. Similarly, there must be resolution of the problems associated with excessive caretaking and selfishness in relationships. These two problems in particular interfere with the chance of having secure and lasting love. They are very common problems, but require specific efforts to limit their negative influences when it comes to lasting love. In addition, learning to recognize even small improvements in love and intimacy can go a long way towards motivating people to continue in their efforts, because the potential payoffs are big. Let's continue with a detailed explanation of the Polarity of Mind Reflex.

Chapter 2

THE POLARITY
OF MIND REFLEX

What You Don't Know About your Brain can Hurt you!

The human brain is designed for survival. You might not think about it a whole bunch, even though we all cart it around everywhere we go. But, we rely on it every minute of the day. In adults, it weighs only about 3 pounds. Within its soupy mass are tissues, structures, liquids and chemicals that work together with our spinal columns to coordinate our lives. The brain can be compared to a series of interconnected programs that communicate with each other and our bodies to support us in daily living. The brain facilitates the meeting of basic biological needs as well as higher levels of functioning. Our brains remind us to take a breath, so our bodies can get the oxygen needed for bodily functions. It reminds us to eat, drink, and sleep. It signals us to be afraid, cautious, or avoid things we perceive as threats. Our brains allow us to feel, think, and act to promote our lives and meet our needs. We are able to move about our environments, drive cars, negotiate business contracts, learn languages, repeat joy producing activities, and reproduce, all because of our brains' activities. To a great degree, our brains have our welfare as its primary focus, to preserve and protect us.

In this book, we are mainly interested in the brain's fight-or-flight response. Most people have heard of it. And most of us can identify times it has been activated within us to help protect us from harm. People mostly think of the fight-or-flight response in terms of protection from physical dangers. Perhaps that was its original purpose when we were forced to defend our survival more often, prior to modern civilization. It is still relied upon at times of danger now, but physical threats are not as prevalent as they were thousands of years ago. Basically, the fight-or-flight response triggers a defensive response where we either attack and fight back to neutralize a threat, or we flee and run away from it. Our physical welfare is therefore protected and our longevity is hopefully guaranteed.

But what happens when the "threat" is an emotional one? That is, what happens when we face a threat to our secure love and attachment with others? For example, what happens to a child's brain when it receives information that his or her needs and feelings don't count, such as through child abuse or neglect? What happens to a young brain when it hears a parent yelling at the child and calling him or her names? In contrast, what also happens within a person's brain when they are treated as extra special or spoiled? What does a spoiled or favored child come to expect in terms of future relationships and mutual respect of needs with others? How are relationships shaped after a person's feelings and related needs are either rejected or overly attended to? (Remember, much of the wiring in our brains related to relationships and survival is formed in our childhood years.)

If we consider having our needs met as basic to our survival, then perhaps the fight-or-flight response and its integrated network of "wiring" throughout our brain has a part to play in the structuring of our most personal relationships. By definition, our "needs" are the specific things each of us finds necessary to reduce a negative state, feeling, or stress; our needs are therefore a means for self-preservation. Similarly, needs can be positive too and help us continue in pleasurable or affirming activities. In essence our needs, both positive and negative, support our survival as humans and individuals. If our needs go unfulfilled, and if we stop and pay attention to how we are feeling, the sensation of negative feelings like anxiety will be evident. The more pervasive we are in ignoring our feelings and corresponding needs, the more likely we are to feel depressed or anxious. Thus, not much good comes from ignoring a biological being's basic needs and feelings.

Another important aspect of needs is that they are based on feelings <u>and</u> defined by our thoughts. In theory, needs per se require a communication between both halves of the brain. Feelings from the right side of brain are interpreted by thinking aspects of the left half; a type of integration of the brain is therefore evident once needs are identified and communicated. In theory, it takes both side of the brain to translate feelings into needs. Perhaps this is why people report a calming effect once they are finally able to identify what their needs are. Our brains like it!

The Polarity of Mind Reflex is the term I use to describe how the fight-or-flight response gets applied <u>interpersonally</u>, in reference to how each person negotiates their needs, and promotes emotional survival through the patterns people engage in with each other. Specifically, the Polarity of Mind Reflex is a model for understanding two compromised solutions to problems often associated with attachment experiences that have gone poorly for any number of reasons. The first solutions include adopting either a self-serving style of relating where a person asserts his/her needs without much concern for others, or an excessively giving style where the person takes care of others without much concern for his/her own needs.

There are psychological terms we commonly use to describe how the Polarity of Mind Reflex manifests itself in relationships and personalities. The narcissist-caretaker pattern is one of them. This pattern is pervasive and presents itself in the offices of psychologists and marital therapists daily. Let's review this pattern briefly. The narcissist, or inherently self-serving person, seeks to get others to meet their needs. Selfish people *covet attention* and their needs typically count more and are at the expense of anyone else's. That is, selfish-types "take" and getting their needs met is something they strive for or "fight" to achieve. They inherently seek to run from the "wound" they try to cover over; their struggle is a deep insecurity about their own lovability and ability to secure love within the turbulent and competitive sea they swim in daily. A sea filled by swells getting in their way of securing enough attention to keep them afloat. You see, attention for narcissists is their life raft. But they see life and relationships in a sink-or-swim fashion. That is, there is only one life raft in their minds for securing any available attention and they want to be in it. But, it is harder to reach shore with just one person paddling and narcissists tend to row their lives (in terms of love relationships) in circles.

In comparison to selfishly-oriented people, caretakers (sometimes called codependents or in more extreme cases victims) structure relationships by giving to others. (Please note that the use of the term "caretaker" in this book applies mainly to people who go about their lives primarily focused on other people's feelings and needs, but not their own. These are people who grow fatigued, depressed, and anxiety ridden as the cumulative effects of ignoring their own feelings and needs accumulates over time. Such people sacrifice their health and well-being all for the sake of other people's happiness. Often, they are bewildered by their own feelings of despondency and related physical depletion and exhaustion as they grow older. Thus, although caretaking by itself is a good and natural way to share in the lives of others, for example when doled out in balanced ways with appropriate attention given to one's own feelings and needs, excessive caretaking is very risky business. If taken to an extreme, caretaking is wrought with extensive negative side effects often unrecognized until significant harm occurs to both the caretaker and the integrity of their love relationships.) Many caretakers never or rarely make their needs known to others. Thus, caretakers "run from" their needs and give extensive attention to other people. Both narcissistic types and caretakers seek to avoid the anxiety and insecurity each feels when it comes to healthier forms of interaction, i.e., where needs exchanges occur and secure love and attachment get created. Each type instead engages in a unidirectional pattern of relating that fails to create a secure attachment with others. Secure love can never be established in either of these two ways. Secure attachment only occurs through mutual respect where both people's needs are voiced and valued. Wow! So that's our problem!

Our Needs and the Polarity of Mind Reflex

In review, the Polarity of Mind Reflex is a concept recognizing the ways the fight-or-flight response affects people's relationships in regards to needs expression. Again, each of the polarities is flawed, because neither results in secure love and attachment. However, because the fight-or-flight response is so basic and integrated in our brain's design, a pattern of relating frequently arises that causes relationship problems that can lead to excessive conflict and divorce. Those who go the selfish route, "fight" to get their needs met. Others' needs don't count to them. In contrast, those who assume caretaking roles "run" from their own needs and seek mainly to structure relationships by being givers. Mutual relating is too anxiety ridden and compromised patterns of association occur. Our brains are structured this way and even though we are no longer fighting or running from saber tooth tigers, relationship polarization is played out in how people fill their needs interpersonally. The Polarity of Mind Reflex represents this dynamic. The end result is two people keeping each other at a distance and avoiding the feelings of anxiety that mutual relating would trigger. Unfortunately, the chances for secure love are lost.

A Note about Anxiety and Intimacy

You might want to stop and ask yourself, why would anyone feel anxious and strive to avoid mutual relating? Why would anyone seek to dominate others and want only their needs and feelings to count in a relationship? Most people recognize that no one wants to be ruled or dictated to. That is not the essence of intimacy or friendship. And yes, it feels good to give and do for others. But what happens to those good feelings when there is no giving back? Furthermore, why do so many people pale when it comes to identifying and expressing their own needs? And why do so many people believe they are acting "selfishly" when they first start to assert needs? There must be something wrong with us as humans, as such problems are pervasive. Problems with imbalances of needs can be seen at the heart of most conflicts between people, be they intimate relationships, friendships, employer-employee pairings or politics. Our brains seem to be working against us.

I think the Polarity of Mind Reflex concept helps to explain why people stay in unhealthy and abusive relationships. As the brain is growing and developing in childhood, neurological pathways are being laid down and embedded in our brains. You might call this process shaping, early learning, or memory formation, but the end result is that children learn whether and how their feelings and needs count early in life. They also learn it at a time when brain development and growth is occurring and neuronal structures are being formed. Right there, along with a child's brain development which is incorporating early experiences is a survival mechanism we refer to as the fight-or-flight response. Applying the fight-or-flight response to our needs, as we did above, we can consider how we learn to fight for our needs (selfishness) or flee from them (caretaking) early in life. I suspect people more extreme in either polarity had complicated or troubled childhoods, where their needs were overlooked, violated, or excessively attended to by a doting parent or person. But once the brain is fabricated and "wired" by the end of childhood, change will not be easy. Patterns of need fulfillment persist until major changes occur such as through psychotherapy.

The need exists to underscore one universal fact about where secure love comes from. Secure and lasting love only develops when the mutual respect of needs exists in a relationship. That is, both people's needs must count in any relationship for trust to be established and secure and lasting love to be created. Stop and reflect on how you cannot trust or be securely attached to anyone, if they regularly disregard your needs. Similarly, if you only meet the needs of others without asking to have your needs met too, insecure and precarious love results. Thus, in relationships neither narcissism (including varying degrees of excessive self-serving behaviors) nor excessive caretaking will ever produce secure attachment. However, our brains seem to forego this because of a more primitive and extensively integrated survival structure. Without knowing it, our brains may be falsely leading us into patterns of relating to others that sabotage our abilities to create secure and lasting love because of the effects of the misapplied fight-or-flight response. Thus, people either learn to run from their needs or want their needs to dominate exclusively, but all at the expense of secure love and attachment. It is no wonder abuse victims stay with abusive partners; their brain's survival structures were shaped early on to do so and this also explains why such patterns are hard to change. For example, it takes time through psychotherapy for the cortex to affect the midbrain and its fight-or-flight composite. What we don't see are all the chemical and cellular wiring configured early in life and integrated into our brain, some of which have been shaped through the fight-or-flight response and how we learn to relate to our needs in relationships. Thus, our childhood experiences affect brain development and can cause reflexive and unwavering patterns of relating which can interfere with the establishment of secure and lasting love.

Below is summarized the presumed steps associated with the Polarity of Mind Reflex and its effects:

STEP 1: A person experiences rejection, abandonment, neglect, abuse, or spoiling. (Or is simply taught to serve and take care of others, but never to consider their own needs.)

STEP 2: The person must survive; children rely on adults for safety, caring, and nurturance.

STEP 3: If parents don't meet their children's needs for security, how will they get met? (Safe and secure love only occurs through the mutual respect of needs.)

STEP 4: The brain automatically directs people towards two groups of behaviors: A. A person focuses on others' needs and assumes a caretaking position in relationships, or, B. They strictly focus on getting their own needs met regardless of the cost to others. (B is also the response when children are spoiled or when the person decides they can't rely on others to meet their needs so they decide to only rely on themselves.)

STEP 5: <u>Mutual</u> respect of needs in relationships is not learned and applied.

STEP 6: Secure love and attachment is prevented. (There is a difference between the feeling of love and having <u>secure</u> love. Simply put, you can love someone or they can feel love for you, but this is separate from being in a secure love relationship. The most obvious example might be that of an abusive husband who loves his wife but beats her…there is no mutual respect here but there are real feelings of "love" shared between them. Always voice and negotiate your needs in a relation-ship. That is the best way for secure love to grow.)

STEP 7: A life course of relationship problems fol-low. People then never experience secure and lasting love. People don't attach well to you because they are unable to practice mutual respect of needs. People leave you or you leave them, because love and attach-ment doesn't get securely established. People wonder why they have to either cope with repeated losses or live their lives never truly achieving secure love. But things can change. They have to, if secure love is the goal.

I want to share one last point about the Polarity of Mind Reflex. People also alternate between caretaking and selfishness. For example, there are times when narcissistic people can be charming and overly attentive to others, but later, once the relationship is more established they shift to their predominant selfish ways. Such is the case outlined in Mary Jo Fay's book *When Your Perfect Partner Goes Perfectly Wrong.* Even narcissists can be attentive to the needs of partners (victims?) in order to seduce them into their web of being "attended to." Similarly, as caretakers seek to become assertive and learn to voice needs they often become very self-focused. Others complain, "What happened to the old you; you seem so selfish now?" Such it is with human nature; people can't help themselves from swinging from one polarity to the other as they navigate needs-exchanges or undergo change. The effects of the fight-or-flight response and its application to needs fulfillment in relationships is habitual and hard wired into us.

I think the Polarity of Mind Reflex helps to further explain complex and persistent relationship patterns. But like any good construct, it can also direct us toward interventions to modify relationship habits that take it into consideration. Briefly, such interventions need to always have as their goal creating the capacity in people to engage in mutually respectful relationships. Problems arise if you only teach a caretaker to act assertively with their partner because this triggers the selfish person's basic defenses; the self-focused individual recognizes a threat to their needs getting met and resistance and conflict will follow. Similarly, if you only try to teach a narcissistic person to be more empathic and to care about the needs of others you will run into problems with their brain and how they learned to only care about their needs as a means to survival. Furthermore, a caretaker's brain also will not easily accommodate to having their needs count as they are habitually much more comfortable taking care of others. Again, mutual interventions are called for here.

Chapter 3

WHAT CAN GO WRONG?

The Trappings of Fear

In the Star Wars series of movies, there is a scene in Episode 1 where Yoda is interviewing young Anakin prior to accepting him as a Jedi trainee or padawan. Anakin asserts his wish to become a Jedi and be accepted to train in a "chosen one" fashion. Yoda, however, astutely points out a glaring defect in Anakin's human armor. Fear exists in his make-up, and too much of it to safely assume he is capable of handling the powers of the Force. Yoda voices his belief that Anakin's fear is at a disabling level, but he gives into others who request/demand for training him against Yoda's better judgment.

As Anakin's training as a Jedi unfolds, it is his fear that entraps him. It is fear that prevents him from having the ability to manage his powers of the Force. Similarly, fear prevents him from having healthy relationships with others. Of note is how an older Anakin, once an adult, engages in domestic violence, nearly strangling his wife Padme to death. Shortly afterwards, Anakin attempts to kill his Master and friend Obi-Wan. Fear (often seen as intense anger and over control towards others) is thus a symptom that something has gone wrong in regards to feeling safe and secure in love relationships. Anakin was removed from his mother at a young age. He later rescues her after she was kidnapped and tortured by marauders. He kills her captors but she dies anyway. His losses are intensified. Thereafter, fear associated with attachment is also magnified. Fear overtakes Anakin and he turns into the evil Darth Vader.

Anakin's experiences illustrate that aggression or rejection is typically associated with an infusion of fear in childhood. Thereafter, the need to control relationships becomes paramount. But this need interferes with the chances of mutual respect of needs and therefore the chances for enduring love. This process can be seen as a type of "human physics:" hurt and rejection cause fear of attachment with others. Fear causes people to become overly controlling in relationships and/or excessively caretaking. However, neither over control or excessive caretaking ever produces secure love and lasting attachment. Love can exist for another person; Anakin like other domestically violent people truly "love" their partners, but without secure forms of attachment including the mutual respect of needs such feelings of love will be squandered. Therefore, we all must be aware of the trappings of fear and work to extinguish them. Even though the way people automatically adapt to rejection tends to protect them in the short run, it interferes with the establishment of enduring love in the long run. This can happen at a more global level, for example, with war serving as a sign that groups have fallen prey to excessive fear and the need for a broader sense of control. The Dark Side of the Force exists in everyone. But so does the need for love.

For readers unfamiliar with Star Wars, there are other terms describing people who have ventured too far into the Dark Side. Terms like sociopath, psychopath, antisocial, and criminal. In all of these types of people, fear and selfishness are incorporated into a lifestyle of defense and control over others. The ability to trust and respect others is gone. Some of these people are so detached from their feelings that hideous crimes are committed. Cheating, lying, and violence color their lives. Mutual respect is the farthest thing from their conscience and relationships.

PROBLEM: Fear and excessive anxiety or worry can be signs that a person is vulnerable in establishing secure love and attachment. Excessive anger and control of others are additional signs of this type of fear.

SIMPLE SOLUTION 1: Fear must be reduced and managed if secure love is to be realized. Attempts to control other people are not mutually respectful. Learn skills to calm your internal self, such as through psychotherapy, relaxation training, meditation, exercise, and journaling. Then you can start communicating and negotiating your needs with the people who matter to you the most.

The Rise of Narcissism

Narcissism is a label associated with extremely selfish people. Narcissism-self love at the expense of all else-is a handicapping condition. But narcissists are the last to realize it. It often takes a life crisis such as divorce or rejection by a loved-one for narcissists to request help for their problems. Such help is too often brief and lasts only until they secure the next caretaker to tend to them. Other ways to address this problem will be discussed later in this book.

In Mary Jo Fay's book, *When Your Perfect Partner Goes Perfectly Wrong*, she describes the narcissist's mindset: "They become blind to reality. They can't see things from another point of view. They forget that others are involved and may be affected by their self-centered decisions." Also in her book she cites commentary from Sam Vaknin, (author of *Malignant Self-Love: Narcissism Revisited)*, an openly narcissistic man who reflects on his views about love. For readers interested in learning more they may wish to read the quote or his book as they describe what many authors have reported in terms of how love and feelings are dismissed, devalued, and undesired by narcissists. Basically, people wanting love and having vulnerable emotions are seen as weak. Given this mindset, it is not hard to imagine the harm narcissists can do to others, whether through criminal behavior or simply by using people selfishly then rejecting them. There is no reciprocity or interest in mutual respect with narcissists, not at first anyway. But, they will never get their concealed need for secure love met acting like this. Again, ideas for helping them will be explored later.

Narcissists come in all shapes, sizes, and ages, male and female. How much narcissism each possesses varies, but they always find ways to turn the focus of conversation and activity back to their needs. They seem to live according to the doctrine: "After me, you come first."

The injuries that give rise to narcissism and a life time of selfishness are varied. Some get that way from being spoiled as children. Parents may not realize the harm they are causing children by spoiling them. Treating children like "king-babies" or prima donnas is like giving them a license to steal love. Everyone knows that stealing is wrong. So why do some parents spoil their children and fail to teach them about mutual respect of needs? Sometimes children who suffer childhood illnesses inadvertently develop selfish habits in life. Spoiling children for any reason can result in an absence of mutual respect for others' needs. Such people become overly demanding of others, never learning the give-and-take required for lasting love and intimacy. Forever they will be frustrated. Selfishness and narcissism never produce the lasting flow of love people need in life--love that will sustain them and keep them healthy. But if selfishness is all you (and your brain) know, you will continue in your efforts forever or until the losses in your life accrue and leave you depressed or criminally compromised in your decisions.

There are other ways to fall into a narcissistic life style. Early losses and rejection can give rise to this condition. If your parent rejects you, you may react by learning to only look out for yourself. Divorce no doubt subjects children to similar challenges in regards to the rejection it entails. Parents not only leave their spouses, but they disrupt the attachment their children receive and rely on. Similarly, if you have a parent who is narcissistic, what you learn from them and repeat in your own relationships can have equally negative effects. If a parent only thinks about his or her needs, you, as their child, will learn to be selfish or engage in catering and excessive caretaking with others. In other words, the currency of attachment becomes polarized. People either progress towards selfishness or caretaking in response to hurt, spoiling, rejection, or abandonment.

Brain development can also be negatively impacted by developmental tragedies in childhood. In the mental health profession, the diagnosis of Attachment Disorder captures the problems inherent in severe abuse and rejection in childhood. Children learn whether the world is safe or not during their early years and perhaps (as some literature suggests e.g., Calkins, S.D. & Hill, A. (2007)) even before in utero. It pays to remember that brain development is occurring in childhood. What children experience in terms of safety, love, and attachment can persist for a lifetime in terms of brain circuitry. Altering brain circuits requires focused and persistent attention and treatment, sometimes across one's life time. It is no wonder that narcissism is so difficult to alter. "Selfish Brain Disease" (SBD), as I call it, is tough to change.

PROBLEM: Both selfishness and caretaking are ineffective in maintaining lasting intimacy and love.

SIMPLE SOLUTION 2: A mutually respectful relationship must be created where <u>both</u> people's needs count.

If Not Selfish, Then a Caretaker You Become

In reaction to rejection in childhood, if a person does not develop "Selfish Brain Disease," a polar opposite problem typically arises. A caretaker they become. But becoming a caretaker is not the solution to life's love problems either. In her book: *The Disease to Please,* Harriet Braiker, Ph.D., describes the debilitating nature of caretaking. Even though it is easier to be around a caretaker because it feels good to be nurtured by them, the caretaker themself is doomed. Giving without ever asking to have one's own needs met is exhausting. Lasting love is not nourished through caretaking, even though it may bring temporary pleasure to the caregiver. Think of anyone you've known who was always willing to help others, but never willing to ask for their own needs to be met. How worn out did they appear? Caretaking without consideration for the caretaker's needs usually results in fatigue, depression, or rejection in life. Mother Theresa may have been an example of someone overcome by the negative effects of caretaking and privately suffered such a fate. In a Biography written my May Gold private letters written by Mother Theresa revealed how she kept secret her years of personal agony and spiritual despair. It is only a matter of time, so it seems, until caretaking takes its toll on people.

Many of the couples I have counseled over the years have demonstrated emotional depletion in one spouse (the caretaker) and a despondency about the lack of love coupled with the willingness to end the marriage in the other (the narcissist). Very often, a narcissistic person will choose a caretaker as a spouse. It may feel like love or even a match made in heaven at first, but this combination is rarely if ever successful. My clinical experience has shown that this common pairing is likely to be a part of the high divorce rate we see in America. Selfish people "need" caretakers and vice versa. But this pairing never produces lasting love and intimacy.

Assuming the strict role of caretaker is fools gold when it comes to establishing lasting intimacy. The caretaker achieves only a "phantom attachment" with their partner. Furthermore, people may stay together, but there is no true sense of lasting love or intimacy commensurate with such pairings that I have witnessed. This is predictable because the human physics of interpersonal attachment does not grow in this way. There must be mutual respect of needs for lasting love or close attachment to grow. The problem is, however, that human beings are inclined to go in one of two directions--narcissism or caretaking--when their early development is impacted by some form of rejection, neglect, or abuse. There has to be a way to try and turn all of this around. And, I think there is.

PROBLEM: Lasting love is not nourished through caretaking, even though it may bring temporary pleasure to the caregiver.

SIMPLE SOLUTION 3: There must be mutual respect of needs for lasting love and close attachment to grow.

Chapter 4

SIMPLE SOLUTIONS TO LIFE'S LOVE PROBLEMS

The Basics

The model I want to present of formulating simple solutions to life's love problems begins with recognition of the need for love and application of the Golden Rule, i.e., mutual respect, in relationships. Both are viewed as essential to healthy human life. Fear is what stands in the way of healthy relationships; it sabotages the possibility of success. Fear can be obvious or subtle in its origins and it needs to be managed, if not removed, in order to open the doors to healthy love relationships. "Life is very short and there is no time for fussing and fighting my friends," the Beatles admonished in their song "We Can Work it Out." But, fear is at the root of love relationship problems. It must be tamed and diminished if simple solutions to life's love problems are to be realized.

PROBLEM: Fear is a primary ingredient in love relationship problems.

SIMPLE SOLUTION 4: Fear must be tamed and diminished if simple solutions to life's love problems are to be realized.

Returning to the Star Wars saga, as Yoda points out to Anakin before Jedi training, the problem with a fear-based existence or reality is the following: fear leads to anger, anger to hatred, and hatred to suffering

(Diagram 1, Choice B). Also, coupled with hatred, and later suffering, is the appearance of "suspicion." Suspicion founded mainly in a feeling and misinterpretation of facts is the precursor to suffering. Once suspicions take root, they are like cancer to relationships. Blame, hostility, and accusations arise and suffering will follow.

Also of importance is the fact that the place of current-day pain is not always where it originated. The effects of childhood abuse and neglect are long lasting. They persist across time, throughout life. Time does not heal all things equally. This is especially true in the case of childhood traumas and severe neglect of children's feelings and needs. Psychotherapy and counseling from licensed professionals are contemporary ways to heal such wounds of the human spirit. Religious and spiritual counseling when administered by mature and healthy individuals offer additional healing. Ignoring the residual effects of early wounds is paramount to casting out hope for a better future. If you want simple solutions to life problems, be sure fear is diminished in your life as well as the residual effects of problems from your upbringing. Time alone does not heal such problems. In fact the needs of most importance to you today are likely similar in nature to the needs unmet in your childhood.

PROBLEM: Early experiences of childhood abuse, rejection, domination, and spoiling can leave a person fearful of secure love and intimacy that is mutual in nature.

SIMPLE SOLUTION 5: If you want simple solutions to life problems, be sure fear is diminished in your life as well as the residual effects of problems from your upbringing.

DIAGRAM 1: THREE LIFE CHOICES AND THEIR RESULTING OUTCOMES

CHOICE A **Mutual Respect**	CHOICE B **Selfish/ Narcissistic**	CHOICE C **Caretaker**
LOVE	FEAR	FEAR
(leads to) ↓ ↓	(leads to) ↓ ↓	(leads to) ↓ ↓
MUTUAL RESPECT	ANGER/ SUSPICION/ HATRED	ANXIETY
↓ ↓	↓ ↓	↓ ↓
CONCERN FOR EACH'S NEEDS	FOCUS ON OWN NEEDS	FOCUS ON OTHER'S NEEDS
↓ ↓	↓ ↓	↓ ↓
TRUST	INSECURE ATTACHMENT	INSECURE ATTACHMENT
↓ ↓	↓ ↓	↓ ↓
INTIMACY/ CLOSENESS	NEED TO CONTROL	NEED TO CONTROL
↓ ↓	↓ ↓	↓ ↓
HAPPINESS	SUFFERRING	SUFFERRING

Of additional importance is to realize that denial and disease are intertwined. Much contemporary medical care is grossly devoid of adequate attention to the psychological components of illness and healing. Certain diseases and health problems can be viewed in terms of their symbolic nature. Bernie Siegel, M.D., in *Peace, Love, and Healing* has suggested there can be underlying feelings and needs represented in a person's health problems that should be considered if medical professionals are truly seeking to be competent healers. Similarly, he points out how denial of feelings and people's inherent need for feeling loved and cared about limits the responses their bodies can put forth to heal them. The mind is connected to the body and can be part of the solution or part of the problem; how you think can intensify or lessen the effects of stress on your body. Hans Selye, M.D. (from book *Mind as Healer, Mind as Slayer, 1977)* indicated this in his work on the general adaptation syndrome. Thus, how a person responds to stress can help or hinder the healing process. With that being said, simple solutions to life problems are more likely if you don't overuse denial to cope with problems whether they are of current or historical (childhood) origins.

PROBLEM: People frequently deny the lasting effects of their childhoods.

SIMPLE SOLUTION 6: Simple solutions to life problems are more likely if you don't overuse denial to cope with problems whether they are of current or historical (childhood) origins.

Starting out with Love or Fear

Let's say there are two life possibilities whose stages are set in childhood. You'll either begin life with love or with fear as your basis for relating to others. Love is the natural inclination for children. With few exceptions, most children are willing to love and be loved freely. If secure love is provided to children, their lives are more likely to progress in healthier ways. Conversely, if "the fear of God" is infused into children through abuse, neglect, and other forms of rejection, love becomes a more complicated process. Infusing children with fear will instill ways of relating throughout their lives that are problematic. This is how bad things happen to good people. Furthermore, problems of childhood that have negatively affected attachment with others will alter the possibilities for healthier relationships in the future.

Let's review a few progressions that follow a love based childhood versus one colored by fear. (Diagram 1) If love is secure and responsibly given to children, they will grow up capable of mutual respect. Mutual respect in relationships is demonstrated through concern for each others' needs. Thereafter, trust is established, intimacy and closeness arise and happiness occurs. In effect, this may be "the secret path to happiness" because it is the trajectory for feeling lasting love. Feeling loved when someone cares about your needs is inevitable. It is hard wired into us all. It's human physics.

PROBLEM: Not everyone gets loved in healthy ways growing up.

SIMPLE SOLUTION 7: Find people willing to love you in respectful ways. Feeling loved when someone cares about your needs is inevitable. It is hard wired into us all. It's "human physics." Sometimes you have to look outside your family of origins to find the love you need.

Lasting love comes from the mutual exchange of needs, however, not from needs exchanges that are unidirectional. Unidirectional love—only taking or only giving—is seen in both selfishness and caretaking. These two ways of relating are flawed because neither produces lasting attachment and closeness. Narcissists and caretakers inevitably experience crisis in their love relationships. Mutual respect of needs is the only way that lasting love can be established.

The outcomes from a fear based development are very different (Diagram 1). When fear is experienced in childhood, that is when rejection or child abuse is experienced, relationships are shaped differently. It is like predestation. If you experience fear that you are not loved in childhood or love is doled out inconsistently or conditionally, it simply messes up future relationships. This is seen as people assume selfish, narcissistic roles in their relationships. Diagram 1 (Selfish/Narcissistic) depicts the angry hostile version of relating, which can arise from abuse, rejection, or spoiling.

In addition to narcissism, fear can also trigger a caretaking role. See Choice C in Diagram 1. Caretaking is in essence an attempt to control love relationships. Yet, it is based on anxiety more so than anger. It is, in fact, "selfish" also because it only includes the caretaker focusing on the other person's needs. Never does the caretaker offer secure attachment to the narcissistic partner, because the caretaker never offers up his or her own needs. Caretakers may seem to be the victims in such transactions, but it is partially due to their own choices. Either way, because selfishness and caretaking are unidirectional patterns of relating, they will not produce secure love for either party. Suffering occurs instead. You can't reach happiness by following either of these two paths. Mutual respect is necessary.

The sources, reasons, and causes of your fears must be dealt with in order for healthier forms of relating to be learned and reliably applied. That is, growth from an anchoring in fear must be replaced with a healthier grounding in love and mutual respect. As Robert DiNiro tells his young son who was befriended by a mobster in the movie "A Bronx Tale," never confuse friendship based on fear for love, they are not the same! The sources and residual effects of your fear must be lessened to pave the way for mutual respect and healthier intimacy to prevail. It's that simple.

A Model for Healthy Relationships: The Pyramid

The Pyramids of Egypt are formidable structures. Their bases are broad and strong. Looking at them gives the impression they will stand forever. The point on top of the pyramid directs us upwards, like a big arrow. It points to the heavens. When we look to the heavens we might be reminded that God sent his only son to us out of love, if that's how we were raised anyway. And secure love is what we all need for happiness and well-being in life. We will use the pyramid as the symbol for a model of healthy relationships.

The pyramid is divided into 3 levels (Diagram 2). At the top is the level of intimacy and lasting love. It is what we are striving for in life and what I want to help you find with this book. Before lasting love can be achieved a level of trust must be established between ourselves and others. Trust is the second level of the pyramid. Trust is necessary for lasting love to be maintained. Simply put, you can't safely love someone who you can't trust. Trust therefore precedes lasting love. But where does trust come from?

Trust arises when the mutual respect of needs exists between people. Therefore, mutual respect is the base and broadest component of the relationship pyramid. Mutual respect, by definition, means that both people's needs count in a relationship. Both people must be able to identify and speak of their needs. Each person must care about the needs of the other person. Both parties must be willing to compromise and take turns if necessary, meeting each others' needs. Lasting love relationships only occur if mutual respect is instilled and maintained.

But you have to know what your needs are to have a chance at lasting love. You also have to care about what the needs are for the other person. Both are necessary. "Please, please me, as I please you," the Beatles sang in the 1960s, and they were right. Now the work begins.

PROBLEM: If someone only receives love in a unidirectional fashion without being taught to also care about the needs of others, it creates flawed love relation patterns.

SIMPLE SOLUTION 8: Each person must learn to care about the needs of the other person.

DIAGRAM 2: THREE LEVELS OF RELATIONSHIP BUILDING:

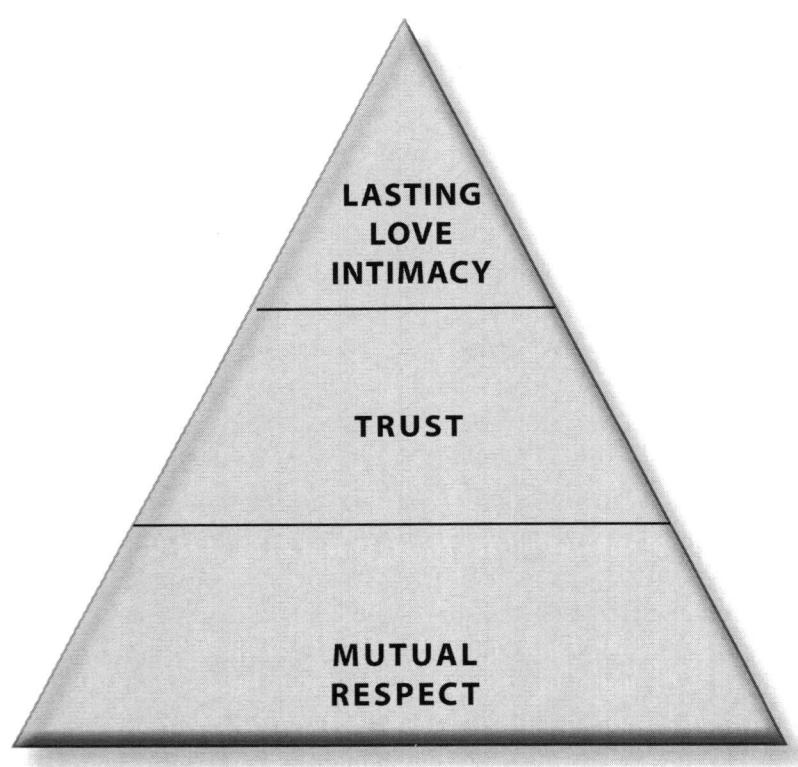

Chapter 5

IDENTIFYING YOUR NEEDS & FENTECC

Your Needs

So, mutual respect is the basis for all healthy relationships. What could be so hard about that? Try this. Pick someone important to you in your life. Sit down with them and do this exercise. Take turns making statements to each other that only begin with one of the following phrases: 1. "I want _____"; 2. "I need _____"; or 3. "I wish_____". Do this for 10 minutes. Each person only makes one statement/sentence at a time. Each statement must start with one of these phrases. Then it is the other person's turn. The Statements don't have to be related to each other. Just go back and forth, like playing tennis or ping pong. Don't start discussing the statements. Just continue to make one of these statements back and forth for 10 minutes. Use a kitchen timer if you want.

Once you have completed this exercise, you will likely notice several things. First, it is not easy to define your needs especially if you are a caretaker. Caretakers offer a unidirectional flow of needs--what can they do for you--hoping you will be happy with them and stay associated with them. In contrast, some people are so self-centered, they can define and express their needs, but can't step away from them long enough to show respect for the other person's needs. Selfish people tend to get irritable or anxious, sometimes calling the exercise "stupid," and resist it for other reasons. Each personality type adds their own piece to troubled relationships and interferes with the establishment of secure love.

Another thing that often appears in this exercise is how hard it is to stick with stating wants, needs, or wishes. Typically, people trail off into statements about their feelings and/or complaints about the other person. People can't seem to help themselves. Ask them about their needs and they speak in code through statements of feelings or complaints. Implied here is the sense that through complaints and feelings the other person should be able to "guess" your needs. Not true. You have to be able to state your needs specifically to another person to start the process of developing secure love.

PROBLEM: People won't know your needs automatically.

SIMPLE SOLUTION 9: You have to be able to state your needs specifically to another person to start the process of developing a secure relationship. Don't expect others to guess your needs without telling them specifically what you want. Also, stop and show interest in their needs too. When you are starting to reshape relationships towards mutual respect you often have to exchange needs with the other person on a 1:1 basis. For example, "I'll do this for you (as you have asked) if you do this for me."

All too often, in marital counseling, spouses portray caretaker and narcissistic pairings that result in a failure to establish lasting intimacy and attachment. Caretakers present as confused, dismayed, and depressed. They don't understand why their spouse complains of no longer loving them. Their spouse might soften the blow by saying, "I love you, but I'm not in love with you." The more self-centered spouse may have found another love interest, relinquishing themselves of the first relationship indicating, "We just fell out of love." Selfish people don't immediately understand what is necessary to maintain "that loving feeling" and neither do caretakers. Relationships are too often doomed with this dynamic, even among couples who remain married. Perhaps this is why the divorce rate is around 40 % for first marriages and higher for second timers. The level and quality of intimacy arising in mutually respectful relationships is much more likely to result in lasting love. Yet, people often get stuck in either caretaking or narcissism and love is little more than a temporary and fleeting aspect of their lives. But what gets in the way of mutually expressing and respecting needs?

There is a misalignment of sorts whereby caretakers confuse their own feelings with those of others. Many of my clients are of the caretaker variety. They are often left by partners who are selfishly oriented or came to therapy dismayed and thinking about leaving themselves. Caretakers often seem to believe that if they just meet their friend or partner's needs, the relationship will be secure. It will not. Human physics demonstrates that lasting intimacy does not occur this way. Mutual respect is needed. But, if a caretaker cannot identify and express their needs, relationship problems are likely to follow and their own happiness will suffer. The book *The Giving Tree* by Silverstein demonstrates problems inherent in parenting of this sort. That is, kids will use you and leave you, blatantly disregarding a parent's needs if all the parent does is engage in a caretaker's role. The same thing happens in marriages or dating relationships. Spouses, girlfriends, and boyfriends don't attach like they should if the expression of needs is unidirectional, that is, if one takes and the other only gives.

PROBLEM: Spouses, girlfriends, and boyfriends don't attach like they should if the expression of needs is unidirectional, that is, if one takes and the other only gives.

SIMPLE SOLUTION 10: Both people's needs must be voiced and respected for secure love to be created.

Three Kinds of People

To summarize, for the sake of simplifying our discussion, there are 3 kinds of people. The first we'll call selfish or narcissistic. Selfish types seem to live according the principle: "It's all about me." They want you to be interested in them, focus on their ideas, and support them in their efforts to get the most out of <u>their</u> lives. Their conversations quickly turn to themselves; they relate anything you say to them and have a short attention span regarding anything about you. They are takers, not givers. You might ask yourself why anybody would want to be like that, when it is so obviously irritating to others. Some interesting solutions for their shortcomings will be discussed later. (For an example, refer back to how Nate Narcissist interacted with his wife in example #1 presented in the Introduction of this book compared with Mike Mutual in example #2.)

The second type of person we will refer to as the caretaker or victim. They focus on the needs of others almost exclusively. They know their role in relationships. They live according to the principle: "Yes, it <u>is</u> all about you." Caretakers are attracted to selfish people, like a moth to a flame. A caretaker and a narcissist each fulfill their complimentary, though problematic, social roles. Moths fly into a flame and disintegrate in the process. So it is for the flame attractant of a narcissist and the insecure identity and anxious attachment of the caretaker. The chance of lasting love for both is incinerated. (Just like how Cathy Caretaker foregoes her own judgment and feelings about her dog, in the example #1 in the Introduction.)

Once caretakers get tired, exhausted, depressed and used up by the narcissist they are easily discarded and a replacement summoned. The replacement, more energetic in caretaking if they've been out of a relationship for a while, may offer what feels like "true love" to the narcissist. However, the pattern is likely to reoccur for there is no secure love without the mutual respect of needs. It doesn't matter how many marriages or relationships you engage in, the narcissist-caretaker pairing is futile in terms of producing a lasting source of love.

The third type of person engages in relationships based on the principle of mutual respect. This person is interested in their needs <u>and</u> the needs of their partner. They are able to express their needs and care about someone else's needs. Compromising and turn-taking is part of their relationships. Lasting love can be theirs, if they find someone else who engages in mutual respect or is willing to learn the skill. (As was the case in example #2 in the Introduction involving Mary and Mike Mutual.)

PROBLEM: Lasting love is hard to find.

SIMPLE SOLUTION 11: Lasting love can be attained, if one can find a partner who engages in mutual respect or is willing to learn the skill.

Getting Aligned with Your Needs: FENTECC

Since selfish people are typically very good at expressing their needs, I will offer some assistance to the caretaker first. Shedding the habits of caretaking should be easy, since it is not a role that brings lasting love. However, letting go of caretaking doesn't happen easily for most people. It's like asking a zebra to change her stripes. So much of a person's identity and social relations can be tied into caretaking, in spite of how much that person may suffer or be stressed because of this role. Simply put, caretakers have to accept that each person's needs must count, including their own, if security and lasting love is their goal.

PROBLEM: Caretaker's attainment of secure love is fleeting.

SIMPLE SOLUTION 12: Simply put, caretakers must accept that each person's needs must count, including their own, if security and lasting love is their goal.

FENTECC (Diagram 3) is a tool used as a guide to help you to identify your needs and to negotiate relationships in an assertive fashion. It is a self-alignment tool. Just like having your wheels aligned in your car, FENTECC supports a straight alignment between your feelings and needs. When a car's wheels are not aligned, navigating down roads can be dangerous. Tires can wear out prematurely. Accidents can happen if your car veers off course and into another's lane. You have to drive more slowly to avoid excessive vibrations in the wheel. Similarly, if people are not aligned with themselves, that is, if their needs are not based on their own feelings but on someone else's, they will not travel the highways of their lives securely. Perhaps the most serious risks they face are a loss of love and attachment with others. They also get pretty worn out and depleted as the years and miles go by without their needs being expressed or met. Thus, FENTECC is a tool for caretakers who get confused and anxious when identifying and expressing their needs in relationships. Furthermore, FENTECC provides you with a roadmap (or GPS) for finding the secure love you need.

DIAGRAM 3: FENTECC: A SELF-ALIGNMENT TOOL

FE = IDENTIFY HOW <u>YOU</u> FEEL

N = USE YOUR FEELINGS TO DEFINE YOUR NEEDS

T = TELL OTHER PERSON YOUR NEEDS (NOT YOUR FEELINGS)

E = EVALUATE WHETHER OR NOT THEY RESPECT YOUR NEEDS

C = CHANGE YOUR THINKING AND BEHAVIOR

C = CONSEQUENCES

The FE in FENTECC stands for identifying how you Feel. It is the first step in the self-alignment process. Caretakers pay close attention. You are to focus on how <u>you</u> feel, not on how others feel. Your feelings are based on what goes on inside you, inside your gut and body, not someone else's. Your feelings are produced by your brain to guide you toward safety, security, and needs fulfillment. Don't worry about selfishness at this point. Selfishness, by definition, means that you only care about your needs, not someone else's. You are extremely unlikely to (ever) only care about your needs if you have lived life as a caretaker. The ultimate goal will be mutual respect of needs. Don't lose your capacity for caring and empathy. It will serve you well later, when you either have a partner or friend that cares about your needs or is interested in learning to do so. Again, the FE is for identifying how you Feel.

The relationship between feelings and thoughts requires discussion. Feelings are not based on how you "think" you should feel. Nor are they based on what others think you should feel. Instead, feelings are based on what your gut and heart "tell you" about the events in your life. It might help if you think of your feelings as sensations you have in your body below your neck line. In addition, if you "think" you should feel a certain way, but do not, then you are in a false alignment with yourself. You may need to work on having courage or more self-awareness, in order to become aligned with yourself and your actual feelings. In Appendix IV I discuss how journaling can be used to enhance your ability to honestly and accurately align yourself with your true feelings and associated needs. Learning to meditate can be a tool useful towards this purpose as well. Thus, learning to be honest in identifying your actual feelings may not be easy. It can be time consuming to start with, but it's worth it if you become more securely attached to people you love.

The N in FENTECC is for your Needs. We'll refer to this next step as application of "Materna's Law #1." According to this law, every feeling you have has a corresponding need or needs associated with it. Your goal, after identifying how you feel, is to link your feelings to your needs. For example, if you feel hungry you need something to eat. If you feel thirsty, you need a drink. If you are tired, you need rest or exercise. Use your feelings to define your needs.

In terms of groups of emotions that cause stress in people's lives, the following pairings of feelings and needs are common. If you feel angry, you need some sort of justice, fairness, or compensation. If you feel sad, you need support, a chance to grieve your losses, a devoted effort to build hope for the future, or self-permission to feel and express anger. If you feel anxious or scared, you need some combination of reassurance, information, or a plan of action/protection (or think of R.I.P. as a way of remembering needs associated with putting fears "to rest.") Every feeling has a corresponding need (Diagram 4). With practice you can learn more specifically what your particular needs are and how to lessen the negative effects of distressing emotions (as well as increase your chances for secure love).

PROBLEM: People often don't know what they need.

SIMPLE SOLUTION 13: According to Materna's Law #1, every feeling you have has a corresponding need or needs associated with it. First identify your feelings than translate them into your specific needs.

DIAGRAM 4: FEELINGS AND THEIR CORRESPONDING NEEDS

Anger = A need for justice, fairness, or compensation

Sadness = A need for grieving your losses, building hope for the future, or giving yourself permission to express anger

Fear/Anxiety = A need for reassurance, information, and plan for action (R.I.P)

As people start to identify their needs and feelings, they typically proceed from general needs to specific ones. Although this is a step in the right direction it can also be problematic. Sometimes you have to work hard at defining exactly what your needs are. For example, you may struggle with worry about your spouse's faithfulness. Let's say they have lied to you in the past and your trust in them was shaken. Your fear is recognized by you and your need becomes trust. "I need to trust you," you might say. However, such general statements about needs can be either too vague for your partner to respond to or they may interpret them as blame. In actuality, you are really voicing a feeling of mistrust and not a specific need they can clearly fulfill. An alternative need, specific in nature, would be to ask them to call you if they were going to be home late from work each day. The latter example is more of a solution to your feelings, in terms of trying to rebuild trust. Thus, the more specific your needs are the better. Specificity also helps you gauge whether you are being treated respectfully and is more likely to support the regrowth of trust. Remember---avoid making general statements about needs because they tend to elicit defensiveness. One person I worked with learned to ask themself the following question: "I feel this way, so I ask myself what need do I have that will make the feeling I have go away." Then verbalize the specific need.

PROBLEM: At first, people state needs too generally.

SIMPLE SOLUTION 14: The more specific your needs are the better. For example, state exactly what you need the other person to do or say.

The next step in FENTECC is T, Telling people your needs. Notice this step does not include speaking of emotions (at this point anyway). The goal here is to first tell people what you need in relationship to them. For example, I need you to stop yelling, calling names, blaming, or ignoring me. I need you to listen to me without interrupting. I need you to stop trying to force me to think just like you. I need you not to threaten to leave me when I speak of my needs. These are all common needs people have when working out conflicts with others.

Why focus on speaking only of your needs, you might ask? There are several reasons for doing so. You are relatively safer telling another person about your needs than your feelings. When feelings are discounted or ignored, it appears to hurt people in deep and profound ways. Feelings are more involved and broader representations of what circumstances mean to us or trigger within us. They are important. However, people seem to be less harmed if a particular need is discounted than if feeling statements are. Thus, for your own safety learn to make your needs known first to people and not your feelings. If the person respects your needs then it is safer to express your feelings to them. I call this Materna's Law #2. If your needs are not respected, be careful how much you disclose your feelings to reduce the chances of getting hurt. It's a little like poker. Your feelings are the cards in your hand. You keep them to yourself. Your needs are the chips or money you place in the pot. You are betting on getting your feelings to count. Does the other person equally match your wagers, that is, do they reinforce your needs by betting equally or a little more? This example may suggest an air of competition, but competition is not intended. The point is, are they in the game with you, respecting your bets, thereby respecting the risks you face putting your needs on the table? And, are they willing to do the same?

PROBLEM: You can be hurt (disappointed) more easily if you only state feelings and not needs.

SIMPLE SOLUTION 15: For your own safety learn to make your needs known first to people and not your feelings. If the other person respects your needs then it is safer to express your feelings to them.

Another reason to voice your needs first and not your feelings is related to what feeling statements sometimes trigger in others. For example, if a person has experienced any degree of childhood abuse or neglect in life they are likely to respond to feeling statements in a personalized defensive manner. This is especially true for histories of sexual abuse.

A study in the *Journal of Marriage and Family Therapy* in January of 2011 by Walker and others indicated just this: "When either or both partners has a history of CSA (child sex abuse), contempt and defensiveness in the couple relationship are greater than when neither reports a history of CSA."

By definition, child abuse and neglect is a rejection of a child's needs and feelings. Furthermore, children often assume responsibility for how parents feel and act. (That's why giving love to children in healthy and responsible ways sets the stage for the child having healthier relationships later in life. Children must learn that their own and others' needs and feelings count.) If a partner or spouse reacts to your feeling statements sharply or with a sense of over responsibility, they are acting defensively. They may try to fix the problem for you but without learning of your actual needs. Or, the other person may deflect to their own feelings and by default reject yours. Thus, conversations can get complicated and deteriorate quickly if you only voice your feelings.

Given the historic popularity of sharing feelings so commonly emphasized in communication skills training, who would have predicted the potential for negative effects of doing so? Abused and rejected people, whether selfish-types or caretakers, do not respond well to statements that are only about feelings. Such statements can quickly trigger a defensive posturing whereby there is no chance for healthier relating. People are similarly sidetracked from the mutual expression of needs and productive problem solving, each of which is necessary to settle disputes and grow closer. Thus, you should lead first with need statements and only thereafter decide if disclosing your feelings is useful.

PROBLEM: People have been misguided through popular advice to tell people how they feel.

SIMPLE SOLUTION 16: Given the historic popularity of sharing feelings, so commonly emphasized in communication skills training, who would have predicted the potential for negative effects of doing so? This should no longer be your first response to others during conflicts. Learn to translate feelings into needs. State your needs. Watch how the other person responds to them. If they care about your needs your feelings are safe to also share. (Needs first. Feelings second.)

Similarly, people mistakenly assume that if they tell someone their feelings then their needs will be obvious. This is often not the case. The needs people have are unique a lot of the time. For example, what helps one person have less fear may not be the same for another person. One person may seek reassurance by asking their spouse when they will be home. In contrast, another person may need a quick phone call as soon as their partner leaves work at the end of the day. This is a good example of how feelings of closeness are engendered between people. Whenever someone meets your needs in the way you define them, you will automatically feel closer to that person. Somewhat similarly, waiters and waitresses no doubt get better tips by paying attention to such details. People like to have their needs met in ways they define. If you don't speak of your needs you miss out on the nourishment and sense of value that doing so can stimulate. Here is also a solution to low self esteem: learn to speak of your needs and associate with people who care about them.

Since a caretaker often fears being selfish, let's review the difference between selfishness and self-worth. Selfishness by definition means that you only care about your needs and not the needs of others. That is neither the goal of FENTECC nor a true possibility for anyone who has a history of excessive caretaking. Self-worth arises when you value your needs, speak of them, get them met, and then demonstrate a willingness to value the other person's needs. You might have to over focus on your own needs temporarily, in order to learn this new skill, but mutual respect of needs is always the goal when it comes to lasting love.

People often report critical comments from others when they evolve from a caretaking role to one of mutual respect. When other people have relied on you to meet their needs without ever considering yours, they will miss the mothering or caretaking you offered them. It can be like withdrawal from a drug. They may protest and cry afoul, wanting the old you back. But unbeknownst to them, your need to assert your needs is directly tied to your survival and achievement of the love you need to become healthy. Persist you must, in spite of others' protests. You will need to explain to them your need to change and help them understand the benefits it will have for you <u>and</u> them in terms of secure love and mutual happiness. There was an old country song with the lyric: "If momma ain't happy ain't nobody's happy!" The same is true for all of us; we simply need our needs to count in our most important relationships.

PROBLEM: When other people have relied on you to meet their needs, without ever considering your own, they will miss the mothering or caretaking you offered them. It can be like withdrawal from a drug for them.

SIMPLE SOLUTION 17: Expect others to be unhappy with you while you are learning to make your needs known. But, explain to them your reasons for doing so and the benefits it will have for both of you.

In summary, the T in FENTECC is simply for Telling people your needs. Again, tell others your needs and be specific. If the other person cares about your needs then sharing feelings should be safer. However, limit the sharing of feelings until you have evidence that your needs count to the other person.

There is one further point to be made about step T. At risk of getting ahead of ourselves, i.e., prior to more fully discussing the phenomenon of narcissism and selfish brain disease in chapter 10, step T actually includes 2 steps when relating to selfishly-inclined people. You can think of the steps as T-1 and T-2. Both pertain to needs statements but have a different purpose. T-1 begins with the word "We." For example, you might be preparing to share your needs with a narcissistic person, but before you do a "We" statement about your mutual needs can be beneficial. Your T-1 statement might go, "We need to work this problem out together." Or, "We need to care about what each of our needs are and seek a compromise." More about "We" statements will be discussed later, but a successful FENTECC must often include two steps and I wanted to point that out now. The reason for the T-1 statement is to try and reduce defensiveness in the mind of a narcissist. They are quick to react to assertive comments from others with marked defensiveness and a refusal to care about others' needs at the expense of their own. Bridging statements that start with "We" provide for an adjustment to the "Polarity of Mind Reflex" (see chapter 10) encountered in narcissists. After the T-1 statement, the T-2 statement is simply a specific statement about the need you are trying to get met with the other person and as originally discussed regarding step T.

The E in FENTECC stands for stopping to Evaluate whether or not the person you are talking to respects your needs. Does this person state they will treat you as you wish and show commensurate changes in behavior? Or, do they instead quickly focus on their own needs and want you to take care of them? The latter response is not what you want; it is not mutually respectful. You may want to stop and ask yourself how important is the relationship to you? For example, if you are asserting your needs to the cash register clerk at the grocery store and they ignore your request for paper bags your response might be different. You might either restate your needs or, the next time, pick a different clerk to check out your groceries. Some decisions give rise to greater choices than others. In contrast, if you tell your needs to your spouse but they ignore them, your choices must be different. Unless you're Elizabeth Taylor, switching spouses may not be so simple. Persistence is the key for relationships that matter most to you.

When you are seeking to assert your needs with a family member, friend, or coworker, learning to repeat your needs is essential. This is one case in life where it is acceptable to be a "broken record." Repeat your needs, but not your feelings. Again, you want your needs to be respected first, to try to protect yourself from having your feelings rejected and being deeply hurt. If you've had previous rejections or hurt from others in your life, you shouldn't need to put yourself at excessive risk. If someone blatantly does not respect your needs, by all means don't state your feelings to them. "Needs first--feelings second," can be considered another rule of human physics to help minimize harm done to you. Furthermore, the less beat up you get in the process, the more endurance you will have as you try to work out conflicts with others.

The first C in FENTECC stands for Changing your thoughts and behaviors. It is very much related to the preceding step E. We will assume the person to whom you are expressing your needs is a person you would like to maintain a relationship with. If they respect your needs, your thoughts might be, "Thanks, I like that, I'll continue to associate with you." That's the easier path to get to go down. Conversely, if they don't respect your needs, your thoughts might be, "No, I don't like this. I don't want to be treated this way." If your feelings are hurt, don't stop there. Avoid resigning yourself to a victim's way of thinking, such as, "Oh well, what do I matter anyway. It's like this with everyone else. I guess I'll just have to look out for myself." It is at this step that adult courses of action are needed, unlike any childhood learning you may have had about your needs not counting. Value your needs. State them again. Believe and act like they matter. More healthy thinking might be, "My needs count too. Not just yours'. I'm going to tell you my needs again." And do so. Repeat your needs. Stay with them. It must be obvious to you that your needs matter if you want to create a lasting sense of love and intimacy in your life. It can be physically and emotionally costly if you don't succeed.

PROBLEM: If others were use to your caretaking, they may reject your needs at first and think you are acting "selfishly."

SIMPLE SOLUTION 18: Value your needs. State them again. Believe and act like they matter.

The second C and last step in FENTECC stands for Consequences. If your needs are voiced and repeated by you, but continuously ignored, consequences are in order. This is not simply a step of punishment for the other person. It is an inevitable byproduct in terms of the human physics of relationships. The consequence will naturally be detachment and distance from people who blatantly disregard your needs. You won't be able to stop it. It is human nature to do so. <u>People just can't be close or intimate to one another if they don't care about each's needs (Materna's Law #3).</u> They can try and be close through caretaking and self-sacrifice, but if they are honest with themselves and not engaging in excessive use of denial, the natural consequence will be distancing from people who disregard your needs.

PROBLEM: People just can't be close or intimate to one another if they don't care about each other's needs. The natural consequence will be distancing from people who disregard your needs. It is an automatic reaction in humans.

SIMPLE SOLUTION 19: Help people learn the importance of respecting each others' needs. Don't reinforce their attempts to have only their needs count. Introduce your needs to them and request that both sets of needs be met.

This is perhaps the tragedy in relationships for caretakers and narcissists. Human physics demonstrates that unidirectional expressions of needs, that is, only giving or only taking, never produce closeness of a lasting kind. Even if people stay married, there will always be a lacking sense about the quality of love and closeness they feel if mutual needs are not voiced and respected. Just reflect for a moment about who you've felt closest to in life. No doubt you could speak freely about your needs to them and them to you. If you have never had such a relationship then there is a newness to discover about what close and enduring love is like. You might be surprised how achievable a closer form of love is. FENTECC can help.

In terms of consequences, therefore, you don't have to make anything up. Once your needs have repeatedly been disregarded you simply have to tell the person their lack of respect is causing you to distance from them. Is this what they want? People may need time to consider the effects of their actions. It might simply be a new awareness for them, especially if they are not used to you having or voicing your needs. Personal decisions have to be made about how much time to give a relationship, before further signs of distancing are realized. Sometimes affairs grow out of this dynamic. All too often people say they enter affairs because their spouses were not meeting their needs. However, the real shame of this is when an affair occurs without the "injured" party ever voicing their needs to their spouse. You can start to see how important the communication of needs is when you consider all the ways relationships can be harmed when mutual respect and the inherent communication of needs is not established.

Divorce or separation can be viewed as the last resort, a final consequence for the persistent and blatant disregard of a person's needs. At some point the debilitating effects of being in a one-way, strictly other-serving relationship become evident. It can deplete your physical and emotional health. It can rob you of the needed replenishing of your health that secure love provides. Ultimately, a person can only take (or give) so much.

As a means of concluding this chapter, let's review 2 examples of FENTECC, one successful and one not. Afterwards, you may want to write the steps down vertically on a piece of paper and practice using FENTECC for yourself to help you get use to using it.

EXAMPLE OF A *SUCCESSFUL* FENTECC:

FE: (To yourself, you are thinking: "I feel hurt (or angry?) by you yelling at me and calling me names.")

N: (To yourself, you identify the needs you have that would lesson your hurt feelings. You want them not to yell at you or call you names.)

T: You tell the other person, "I need you not to call me names and to stop yelling at me."

E: You observe as they lower their voice tone and you hear them apologize to you for calling you names. They seem to respect you.

C: You change your thinking and behavior regarding them. You think they are showing you respect. You will continue to talk over your problems when they arise and seek mutual solutions.

C: No consequences are needed.

EXAMPLE OF AN *UNSUCCESSFUL* FENTECC:

FE: (To yourself, you are thinking: "I feel worried that you will leave me. You threatened to do so every time I get upset about you staying out late drinking with friends at the bar.)

N: (To yourself, you are thinking: "I need you to stop threatening to leave me. I also need you to come home after work to help the kids with their homework.")

T: You tell the person: "I need you to come home after work and help me and our kids with their homework. And I need you to tell me you will stay and work things out together."

E: However, you laugh at me. You tell me to not be a party-spoiler and you tell me I am stupid and show me no respect.

C: I change my thinking about you. I start to think you really don't care about my needs. Partying seems to be your first concern. However, I love you. We have 3 kids together. But now I will persist and voice my needs (behavior change) again because I know my needs must also count if I am to be in a secure love relationship.

C: (To yourself, you are thinking: "I am worried that you will never show that you respect my needs too. I fear that more severe consequences will be needed in the future. I notice I don't feel real close to you right now…)

Chapter 6

THE IMPORTANCE
OF CONFLICT

What is "conflict"?

Although conflict is often thought of as something bad by most people, it really shouldn't be. Conflict is vital to any intimate relationship. It ranks right up there with people's sexual relationships in regards to building intimacy and fulfilling important life needs. Conflict may be stressful, but many of the reasons for this can be managed or lessened. The Polarity of Mind Reflex helps put conflict into a different perspective and underscores the inevitability of it. Conflict usually arises when there are differences of opinion, conflicting values, needs, or feelings. But conflict doesn't have to be avoided. In fact, it shouldn't be if both parties want to have a secure relationship with each other. Conflict with others is purposeful. It allows for normal mutual association to occur. That is, conflict is an opportunity for intimacy, friendship, and attachment. It can be a "sheep in wolf's clothing," if it is handled well.

How conflict is managed by any two parties will determine whether closeness or friendship develops, versus animosity and "enemy hood." Nowhere is this more important than when starting to modify relationship problems associated with the Polarity of Mind Reflex. In Chapter 9 I will present a 4-stage model of conflict resolution that anyone can apply. The model is a tool to guide and direct simple solutions to life's love problems. But before presenting the conflict solving model, several important issues and other tools will be outlined. Each issue or tool helps you understand problems people frequently encounter dealing with conflict and give you ways of managing them. Again, it is best to know why you are using the tools in this book, so that you can have faith in them. They must make sense to you to get the most benefit from them. Furthermore, being skilled in dealing with conflict is vital to building and maintaining healthy love relationships. The more tools you have at your disposal that support the mutual respect of needs, the better.

PROBLEM: Conflicts are more risky when either party rejects the other's needs and considers them as unimportant.

SIMPLE SOLUTION 20: The more tools you have at your disposal that supports the mutual respect of needs, the better.

Barriers to Conflict Resolution with Lovers and Friends

First, let's consider why conflict is so often avoided. We can get to the heart of this matter very quickly. Just ask yourself, when you were mad at someone for how they treated you, why didn't you say something to them? Why didn't you ask them to change how they treated you? You were probably anxious and afraid of their response. Notice how quickly "fear" arises in your response to conflict resolution. Fear, and its nervous system underpinnings commonly labeled as anxiety, is at the root of our problems. Fear derails us from speaking up, making our needs known, and resolving problems. Fear, by default, also disables us from being close to people and establishing a durable love relationship. But what in the world are we afraid of? We are only talking about telling someone to treat us differently. What is so threatening about that?

A couple of fears are commonly reported by people who avoid conflict. One is fear that the other person will get mad at them. Here we immediately see how an individual's self-alignment is quickly compromised. People too easily let go of their feelings, and thus their needs, and misalign themselves with the other person's potential anger. This is, unfortunately, the plight of caretakers. Afraid that someone will get mad at them caretakers give in and reject their own feelings and needs. And herein lays the problem. If you only align yourself with the needs of others you might avoid the anxiety of conflict but you miss establishing a lasting sense of love in your life. Turn your back on your own feelings and needs and there is no chance for a lasting closeness with others. However, if you are afraid the other person will physically hurt you, that is another story and requires that your needs for safety and self-protection override your need to assert yourself in other ways. But assuming the absence of physical danger, staying aligned with your feelings and needs will facilitate attachment and lasting love more than letting the other person's needs always dominate your own.

Another fear people have when it comes to conflict is the fear of rejection and abandonment. This is especially true for caretakers. This is equally true for adults who as children experienced rejection of their needs on a regular basis. People are sometimes coached into believing their needs don't count in life. Women, even in today's modern society, are still too often taught to only look out for the needs of others and ignore their own. Men also receive similar messages and become caretakers too. Another common sentiment is voiced when some parents assert that children "should be seen and not heard." All are big mistakes. You want yourself and your children to be seen <u>and</u> heard. Adults and children need to be able to say, "Stop, you are hurting me." They also need to say, "I need you to treat me differently, and here's how...." Silence is not golden when it comes to mutual respect of needs and establishing secure love. You have to speak up.

PROBLEM: Children's needs are too often ignored.

SIMPLE SOLUTION 21: You want you and your children to be seen <u>and</u> heard. Adults and children need to be able to say, "Stop, you are hurting me." They also need to say, "I need you to treat me differently, and here's how...."

A related point in regards to raising children pertains to a previously common but misguided belief that "respect must be beaten into children when they misbehave or mistreat others." It is never a matter of, "spare the rod, and spoil the child." Children aren't spoiled because you don't beat them. Kids are spoiled if you don't take time to show them that their <u>and</u> others' needs count in life.

If you have been living life as a caretaker, you will need to be ready to cope with others who may resist your efforts to change. Some people complain that caretakers have "gone crazy," once they start to speak of their needs. But you have to remember where secure love comes from. It only comes from mutual respect of needs. That's the simple truth. It's all there is to it. But give others time. In order to achieve a more permanent love, you will have to persevere through the resistance you will hear and experience from others. After all, they mistakenly were taught you were there to meet their needs not yours.

In many cases, caretakers often have to switch to a self-serving way of relating at first in order to become aware of their needs and express them. You must have faith in what you are doing along with the courage to persist. Don't be surprised if others call you the most dreaded name a changing caretaker can be called: "selfish." Selfish you are not. Not permanently anyway. Having needs and voicing them does not mean you are a "bitch" as some may call you. It is normal to have needs. Don't let selfish tendencies in others derail your path to success. We will later discuss how to limit negativism and blame from others, for example, if you are dealing with someone who is more selfishly-oriented or narcissistic. For now, remember the key to human happiness and secure love only comes through mutual respect of needs (Diagram 5). Fighting the desire of others to assert their needs over your own is part of the territory you will be travelling through, until others learn to relate to you differently. It is for your and their own good, in terms of establishing secure and healthy love that you must learn to make your needs known.

PROBLEM: Caretakers struggle to voice needs and suffer with false feelings of selfishness.

SIMPLE SOLUTIN 22: Caretakers often have to switch to a self-serving way of relating at first, in order to become aware of their needs and express them. Remember, it takes time for your brain to change and you will feel some anxiety and confusion as it does.

DIAGRAM 5: KEY TO HAPPINESS

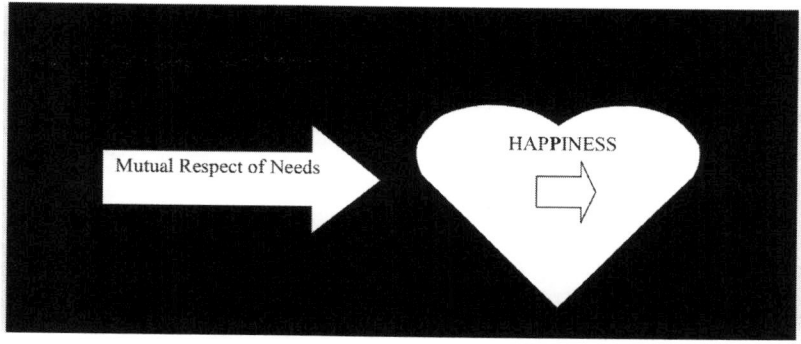

Chapter 7

CONFLICT TOOLS

Countering Blame and Guilt with Kung Fu

Verbal attacks often are in the form of blame and guilt ridden statements. The following list shows some examples:

- "It's your fault!"
- "How can you act like that?!"
- "Me, what about you…?"
- "If you wouldn't do that, I wouldn't feel like this."
- "You're to blame, not me."
- "All you ever do is complain!"
- "I can't do anything right!"
- "You never take responsibility for anything."
- "Why is it always my fault?"

Have you heard or said any of these things before? You are not alone. These are all common statements in defense of oneself. Interpersonal self-defense takes different forms, with communication being one of them.

Have you ever noticed what happens after you say or hear one of the above statements? Not much good, that's for sure. Blame and complaining reflexively produce additional defensiveness in others. There are typically no solutions that arise from such exchanges. Instead, mutual anger and frustration flourishes. And the conflict goes on, unsettled with no solutions set forth to resolve the problems. What simpler alternatives are there? The polarization of needs related to the Polarity of Mind Reflex requires tools and skills to counter them.

The following tools to diminish blaming and complaining in conflict were influenced by a comment I heard several years ago from Kung Fu master Sifu Nick Gracenin. We were talking in his class about people saying mean things to others, such as kids in school. Sifu Nick didn't hesitate saying, "You have to say something; you can't just walk away silently all the time." I thought about his words for quite a while. What about ideas like "turn the other cheek?" Or, "just ignore them." If it wasn't for the fact that the human brain doesn't do well with perceiving it is being victimized, perhaps silence might be golden. But this does not appear to be the case with verbal conflicts or attacks. The human brain needs to know the person tending to it is not taking on the role of victim. Your brain must hear you speak up for yourself.

PROBLEM: People do not respond well—internally—when they act in demeaning self-effacing ways. As time goes on, symptoms of depression and anxiety accrue.

SIMPLE SOLUTION 23: The human brain needs to know the person tending to it is not taking on the role of victim. <u>Your brain must hear you speak up for yourself.</u>

But, what do you say? What do you get out of saying something versus silence? I thought about this. I was certain Sifu Nick knew what he was talking about. He had studied a long time with Chinese masters and knew a lot about self-defense. It dawned on me that you don't have to call the other person names, yell at them, or scream. (Certainly, don't complain about how they make you feel!) Instead, there are some simple and brief statements you can make to defend your own internal sense of worth. These will be explored in the following paragraphs. They are designed to maintain what your own brain registers, or hears, in regards to your self-worth. Ultimately, they are *for your ears only*;

you are not to care about how the other person responds to you in these situations, that is, when the other person still seeks to dominate you and ignore your needs entirely.

The Simple Power of "No"

What should you specifically do, in response to others blaming you? First, there is a lot of power in simply using the word "no." It is a great word and can help mentally signal to the other person something is wrong and further listening is in order. Like Nancy Reagan, wife of deceased President Ronald Reagan, used to say in regards to illicit drug use: "Just say no." Sometimes simple is best. There doesn't have to be extensive discussions, especially if the other person is not willing to listen to you or doesn't care about your needs. Some people just don't care about others' needs and may never be willing to do so. But the word "no" is powerful. It stops people psychologically, at least for the moment, to recognize you are not easily relinquishing yourself to their control. You might simply stop talking after telling them "no," for now anyway, to return and negotiate needs another day. Or, simply end the conversation, but leave a message, mostly for your ears to hear, that you don't agree with them. Sometimes just saying the word "no" is like a verbal punch in the nose for the other person. You simply don't agree. You walk away, keeping control over your self-worth.

PROBLEM: Some people will quickly reject your needs. They simply seek to dominate you.

SIMPLE SOLUTION 24: The word "no" is powerful. It stops people psychologically, at least for the moment, to recognize you are not easily relinquishing yourself to their control.

A good follow-up after saying "no" is saying "I don't agree." It serves as a 1-2 punch in support of <u>your</u> self-worth. Again, what you hear yourself saying is more important than whether the other person acknowledges your words. In this way you retain the control and power over your self-views, and your brain gets to hear you doing so, which it will like a lot! The great advantage of this approach is that it lays the groundwork for the other person to start to consider you as less of a victim during future conflicts. Just keep at it. Don't stop. Do not return to a caretaker's path of self-dismissals and misalignments.

PROBLEM: People stay silent because they know the other person doesn't care about their needs... "What's the use?" they often tell themselves?

SIMPLE SOLUTION 25: What <u>you hear yourself saying</u> is more important than whether the other person acknowledges your words. Always say "no" out loud so you can hear it and "I don't agree." Then, just walk away for now.

Stating Your Needs

Another tool for dealing with blame is to directly state your needs. The two statements: "I want_____," and, " I need _____," are better choices for dealing with conflict than telling others how you feel. Less is also more. That is, the less you say the better, especially if you do not feel listened to by the other party. If the other person is limited in their capacity to listen to you, make sure what they hear is your needs and not a statement likely to generate defensiveness, such as how they make you feel. When all else fails, state your needs and go. I realize this is different than common relationship advice, specifically going against telling people how you feel. What you have to remember is <u>only</u> telling a person how you feel leaves you more vulnerable to being hurt. In fact you are assuming too much, e.g., that the other person will know what you need just by telling them your feelings. This is a flawed way of thinking and relating. People often don't translate your feeling statements into needs that are likely to match those that will settle your feelings for you. In addition, if the other person doesn't care how you feel or is too upset in the moment to listen, your feelings will be ignored and you are likely to feel more hurt. Thus, if conflict is intensifying or the other person is not taking time to listen to you it is better to clearly state your needs and then stop the conversation. At least for the time being. Let your needs be the last thing spoken of not your feelings, because your needs are the solutions to solving your problems. But don't forget, your feelings are important to you. They privately (in your mind) guide you to what you need and must be considered when settling conflicts with others. (Materna's Law #1: every feeling has a corresponding need or needs associated with it.)

PROBLEM: People persist with ignoring your needs.

SIMPLE SOLUTION 26: When all else fails, say "no" then state your needs and go.

Are You Being Listened To?

I wish to restate that it is always important to pay close attention to whether you are being listened to or not. If you are not being listened to, stop and consider your choices. If you are not being heard, there is not much good in continuing to "talk" with the other person. A first task may be to ask to be listened to. After all, your goal is to voice your needs and this is a primary one at this moment. However, some people absolutely refuse to listen or care about what others have to say. From my point of view, if this pattern persists, your love needs are very unlikely to get met. This is when psychotherapy and counseling can be helpful, especially if you want to give the relationship more time to try and overcome this fundamental communication deficit. Usually it is a good sign when your partner recognizes your shared communication problems and is willing to go together for help. But if they refuse to go with you and persist at not caring about your needs, it raises the question regarding how long you should keep trying. Unfortunately, sometimes in life you have to deal with alternatives like separating or ending your relationship with them. There are no easy answers to such dilemmas, but you get to decide how long you want to persist with such relationships and whether it is time to break free from them or not.

Avoid Making Defensive Comments

Avoid defending yourself with people who use blame and criticism in their conflict with you. I know this is hard to do, but try you must. If you defend yourself with someone who is not willing to listen to you, it is a waste of time. It also contributes to you assuming a care-taker or victim role. Verbal defense to a person not willing to listen to you simply gives them power over you. Furthermore, it removes you and them from getting to the task of voicing needs and establishing mutual respect.

Izzy Kalman, M.S., Director of Bullies to Buddies, Inc., has a great question to ask yourself in response to others blaming or being critical of you. I heard this question while attending a conference he was giving several years ago. Simply ask yourself, "Is it true?" That is, is it true what the other person is saying in your mind? Most likely it is not. Remember this. Izzy's question in response to blame or insults further supports what I have suggested in the application of FENTECC. You have to be aligned with yourself and not the views of others when it comes to defining yourself. You should work to never give others the power over you to determine your feelings, thoughts, or needs. They have no right to do so. Don't let them. This is a major point for caretakers seeking to define better boundaries between themselves and others.

PROBLEM: Some people will be persistent about wanting to dominate you.

SIMPLE SOLUTION 27: Never give others the power over you to determine your feelings, thoughts, or needs. Work to define you own reality for yourself!

Another question to consider for yourself, in response to blame, is, "Are you more limited by how you have been treated in life, or in what you have learned?" Let's assume, like a lot of people you have had some unfortunate experiences growing up or later in life. You may have been rejected, abandoned or abused in some way. Just as a stopped clock is always right twice each day, some blame may be valid with regards to mistakes you have made that arose out of problems you experienced in your attachments with others. But don't stop there. Don't let accusations by others cause you to respond defensively. You get to decide your actual self-worth or the nature of your character--based, hopefully, on what you have learned along the way in life. You don't have to be defined by bad events. They affected you, but what did you learn from them? Don't let bad life events or others' blame stop you from applying tools and knowledge designed to get you back on track. Your goal is to establish secure sources of love, and nothing should stop you.

In review, you have to know what to say to the other person, instead of defending yourself. Other responses include just saying "no," and/ or, "I disagree," as well as, "I want_____," I need_____," "I wish_____." If the other person refuses to listen to you, stop talking with them. Walk away. Don't stay in a conversation if the other's views are the only ones to count. It is not good for you. It is toxic to growing secure love in your life.

Loud Voices: What They Are Really Saying

The saying goes that, "Shallow brooks are noisiest." So it is with people. People yell or raise their voice when they want to try to dominate you and are feeling a loss of control. In a way it is a sign of vulnerability and weakness. It is similarly a sign of fear. Yes, yelling is a sign of fearing a loss of control. It shows worry and frustration about not feeling heard or secure in a relationship.

There will be less need for yelling if both parties work to make specific needs known. When someone yells at you, you can tell them you need them to lower their voice. In addition, you can ask them what they need. A lot of times people don't even realize what their needs are or mistakenly think that by yelling or expressing feelings you will guess their needs. Not likely! It is easier to work on asking about needs and working to translate general statements about needs into more specific ones. Again, anger is "code" for at least 3 needs: the needs for justice, fairness, and compensation. Sometimes, the quickest way to lessen someone being angry at you is to interrupt them and ask them, "What do you need?" Repeating this question is a better tool to use when being yelled at than yelling back at them. You can learn to use language to dismantle hostility and facilitate better problem solving.

PROBLEM: People's anger can get out of control.

SIMPLE SOLUTION 28: Sometimes, the quickest way to lessen someone being angry at you is to interrupt them and ask, "What do you need?" Or, "What would make things better for you?" Repeating these questions are better tools to use when being yelled at than yelling back at them.

When you interrupt an angry person and ask them what they need, be careful about one thing, particularly if you have been a caretaker with them. Do not ask them, "What can I do for you?" or, "What do you want me to do to help?" These types of questions are counterproductive.

You are reentering caretaker's land and should avoid doing so. These questions are too close to having you assume responsibility for the other person's problems. It's not a good thing to even imply. The slope back down into the pit of over responsibility for caretakers is slippery and easily fallen back into. Even though the other person will have things they need you to do, let them tell you what they are. Don't imply how badly you want to be helpful to them. It is more important to let them take full responsibility for defining their needs, not you.

Men also can use their loud voices to overpower women. Of course women can have loud voices too, but the voices of men and their testosterone support them in using voice tone to communicate anger (which as we learned earlier, is really about their fears). Thus, women need to be prepared to apply the above strategies with men to draw attention to their needs. Men certainly are not lacking in the need to dominate and control others. However, men need to increase their ability to identify and voice needs too. There will be less need for them to yell if they do.

Calm Yourself Down and Take a Minute (or more)

Just in case it is not clear already, you have a nervous system with a fight-or-flight response and it wants to "protect" you at all costs. However, we all have to be careful. Our feelings associated with protecting and defending ourselves can get out of control quickly. You know you are starting to react internally in an unhelpful way when you notice you are not listening to what the other person is saying. Furthermore, if you feel the need to interrupt the other person before they can finish what they want to tell you, you are probably losing control over your nervous system. If you wait too long to stop and take a break to calm yourself down, adverse effects can occur to your relationship with the other person. You need to have a way of pulling yourself back-in so you don't overreact and say or do things you regret.

People who practice meditation on a regular basis seem to have a leg up on the rest of us. They practice progressive relaxation and focusing/refocusing of their minds, allowing them better control over themselves. Meditation harnesses the life-enhancing benefits of deep and relaxed breathing. If you are able to pay attention to your breathing and learn to breathe more deeply and also refocus your mind off of fight-or-flight demands, conflict management becomes much easier. Thus, if I could wave a magic wand, all of us would be able to stop and relax ourselves on as-needed basis by breathing in, breathing out, and calming our minds. If you are interested but haven't tried or learned to meditate yet, give it a try. Look for classes in your area. (See references by Lucas and Siegel & Kornfield in back of this book.)

Some readers may already understand their need for time-outs during arguments. Things start to get intense, voices rise, words start to fly, and hurt or bruised feelings occur. Try not to blame the other person for all that you are feeling. And you should stop talking; once listening stops not much good is likely to happen with further "conversation." You might have an emotional land mine you didn't know of that the other person mistakenly triggered (more about emotional land mines in a little bit). But it is essential that you have a way to calm down. This usually means walking away for a while. If you have to take a break, try and reassure the other person that after you calm down you will return and try and settle your problem together. But be sure to return later, when calm, and negotiate your needs together.

Some people like to use exercise or another activity to get their minds off the problem. If you do these things try and not obsess about what you don't like about the other person or repeat thoughts to yourself about what they did that annoyed you. Try and think of your needs and how you can communicate them in the future. Whether using meditation, exercise, or another activity to help calm your nervous system, paying attention to your breathing and your self-talk (what you let your mind dwell upon) are helpful. Deep breathing calms your nervous system and thinking about your needs and the possible needs of the other person are similarly useful. I've spent a lot of time "underwater" swimming through problems and absorbing the calming effect the laps have upon me. But I also know I have to be thinking in helpful and balanced ways. What works for you might be different. Perhaps prayer is your form of calming yourself. The nice thing about prayer and meditation is that both are free and you can do them almost anywhere and anytime. (Journaling, as outlined in Appendix IV can also have a similar effect upon your nervous system if you follow the activity as outlined.) So learn to identify your signs that your nervous system is engaging its fight-or-flight system. Stop and take a break. Calm yourself. Assess your needs. Then renegotiate your needs collaboratively with the other person.

The Chi (Interpersonal Power) of "We"

Continuing with a Kung Fu mindset, dealing with conflict can be done effectively through utilization of martial art skills and applying them to communication. For example, during Kung Fu class, Sifu Nick Gracenin taught simple ways to efficiently respond to an attack. He used to say that kids' best weapon was to use their voice and yell for help, especially with an adult who was bigger and more powerful than them. In addition, he also demonstrated physical means to respond to someone's actions when they are trying to harm you. Chinese martial arts, like good verbal conflict management, seek to utilize what the opponent or other person does to you in such a way to help them stop aggressing. Chinese martial arts, generally speaking, seek to make peace with an enemy, by defending yourself physically and using an attacker's physical motions against them. In this way, people who are attacking you are compromised in part through their own actions towards you. You use their efforts to succumb them, since every action they take leaves them open to an alternative attack or response from you. Similarly, the goal in verbal conflict is always the mutual respect of needs. This is the end point you hope for as you try to verbally make peace with someone who is treating you like an enemy. You use your words strategically to coax them towards mutual respect. This is where the power inherent in words like "we" can be realized.

The tool I am introducing here will also be discussed in the chapter dealing with narcissistic people. Because the tool is important in managing conflicts between people, I want to preview it here. However, it is especially relevant when responding to selfish or narcissistic types.

The tool is one of unity. Using words like "we," "us," and "our'" introduces an aspect of relationship building easily overlooked in the mutual struggle to get one's needs met. At the heart of this tool is the idea that people need secure love in life, but they don't always know how to get it or speak of it. Again, as discussed in chapter 2, people's brains reflexively polarize between being selfish or being a caretaker, but neither brings lasting love. This is even more evident in people who have been traumatized, neglected, or spoiled in childhood. Words of unity, like "we," " us," and "our," especially help selfish people's brains realize that mutual respect is intended, and not an attack to cajole them into a victim's role where only the other's needs count. That is the trouble with assertiveness alone. Being assertive is necessary but not sufficient for negotiating lasting love and intimacy. Selfish people resist assuming a victim's position at all costs. This is why only asserting your needs with them may not bring about the mutual respect needed for secure love. Instead, it triggers a psychological battle within them that is not good for either of you. You have to introduce terms of unity. Words like "we," "us" and "our" offer a bridge toward collaboration that assertiveness alone fails to do. People with selfish brain disease need to hear such statements to help defend themselves against ingrained fears of becoming victims too. Assertiveness alone triggers defensiveness in selfish people and a battle of whose needs will count. Again, selfish people believe "better you than me" when it comes to victimization and caretaking, but this thinking must be combated if the chance for secure love is ever to be realized.

PROBLEM: Just stating your needs (alone) will often trigger defensiveness in people prone to selfishness and domination.

SIMPLE SOLUTION 29: Being assertive is necessary but not sufficient for negotiating lasting love and intimacy. You need to attend to joint concerns and shared needs. The words you choose to use can make all the difference when it comes to shaping a relationship towards mutual respect.

An example of communications with a selfish person about mutual needs might include statements like: "No. I don't agree." "We need to _____." Then adding, "<u>We</u> have to respect each other." Or, "It is not good for <u>us</u> to fight like this." And, "<u>Our</u> children need to see us getting along better." Even if the other person won't listen to you, it is still good to use these language tools with them before ending your conversation. Selfish people need to hear words that indicate they are not going to be victimized, discounted, or made into a puppet. They fear such a fate more than most people realize. The underlying assumption is that they don't know how to have lasting love either. Therefore, if the person is important to you, strategic communication and perseverance is needed. Give your words time to sink in to their brains and use mutual language as much as possible.

PROBLEM: Selfish/narcissistic people don't want to be dominated either.

SIMPLE SOLUTION 30: Selfish people need to hear words that indicate they are not going to be victimized, discounted, or made into a puppet. Leave them (and their brains) with the experience that your goals are mutual in nature and you have no intention of dominating them. That is, use words like "we," "us," and "our."

Perseverance and Not Cutting Off

An attitude adjustment may be needed on your part to increase your chances of success dealing in conflict with others. A couple of questions to ask yourself are: How important is this person to you? And, do you want to try and be close with them? (Remember FENTECC.) If you do, and you understand and get good at applying the tools in this book, then remember that changing people's fears about love and closeness takes time. But you don't want to retreat to a caretaker's role. Mutual respect is the goal. Patience is needed, but only if being patient includes a plan of action to get you what you want and need too. That's what the tools and information in this book are for. However, there are no guarantees in relationships. It is sometimes better to end a dysfunctional relationship when your needs have no value to the other person. But, this should not be your first response given your need for secure love in life. The choice must be left up to each person in deciding when "enough disrespect is enough," but perseverance with new tools can sometimes bring surprising results.

PROBLEM: Some people refuse to let your needs count—ever!

SIMPLE SOLUTION 31: It is sometimes better to end a dysfunctional relationship when your needs have no value to the other person and you get the sense they never will. But don't be afraid to give the new tools described in this book some time to work.

After a fight or blow-up with another person, when trying to work towards secure love, it is important <u>not</u> to avoid contact with them. Be prepared and ready to use the tools of communication discussed in this chapter. Your next contact has the chance of being different with them. You'll never know when a small change will occur. If you avoid the other person you may never get to see changes they are starting to make. I have seen surprising changes start to surface between people who engage in conflict when mutual respect is embedded in their communication skills, in spite of how upsetting their arguments were. How you "fight" with people matters. Using skills associated with "making peace with your enemy," and guided by the mutual respect of needs, can produce results other approaches don't.

Learning to Talk to Yourself

Self-talk is an important part of your change process. What you tell yourself matters in terms of reinforcing a sense of victimization or empowerment. When you don't want to cut-off from someone, and you accept the need to work through conflicts, consider different self-statements and how they make you feel when defining a course of action. For example, let's say there are 3 tiers of power represented in the following three statements. The first is to say to yourself, "I avoid them." What is that like? How does it make you feel about yourself? Does it trigger feelings of confidence or cowardice and weakness? Next, say to yourself, "I stay away from them." How does that feel? It has a little more intention and feels slightly more powerful than the first. But, it still tilts toward avoidance and passivity. Now, say to yourself, "I won't let them." What's that like for you. Do you feel and notice the difference? This last statement is more empowering than the other two. Which do you think you should be saying to yourself? Self-improvement is a gradual process, so you may initially be more comfortable with the first or second statement. However, your goal should be self-talk including the last statement, "I won't let them," when it comes to not letting others mistreat you or define your reality. Work on keeping your mind focused in a power-reinforcing direction.

PROBLEM: Others may prefer that you stay in a "victims" role.

SIMPLE SOLUTON 32: Your goal should be self-talk including the statement, "I won't let them," when it comes to not letting others mistreat you or define your reality.

Who Defines Reality?

Who is in charge of defining reality when it comes to the facts, points, meanings, and feelings associated with conflict? For example, is it the bigger, taller, prettier, louder, or wealthier person? The fact is **_no one should be allowed to define reality for the other person when it comes to love relationships_**. Love must be based on mutual respect, that is, mutual realities having shared value. In spousal abuse one person, often the husband defines reality for his wife in strong-handed ways. He may threaten his wife, strike her, or withhold money and resources. Or, one person may interrupt, ignore, and change the focus back to them as a means of not respecting the other's reality and needs. Thus, there are obvious and somewhat subtle ways another's reality can be deemphasized. The problem is that a weaker attachment arises between both parties, especially when fear of rejection is thrown into the mix. Some people "fight dirty" at times. However, you can be wiser and recognize the futility of talking to someone who doesn't care what you have to say. You can also apply the tools in this book to attempt to improve the degree of mutual respect in the relationship and security you seek. You might also decide you have had enough disrespect from the person and end the relationship entirely.

Conversely, it is also important to not try to change the other person to think or feel just like you. That violates the code of mutual respect. In the movie *Pirates of The Caribbean: Curse of the Black Pearl*, the pirates speak of "The Code." Even evil handed pirates had a code (in the movie) they followed that allowed others to voice their opinions to the captain of a ship. "Parle!" they'd exclaim, and expect to have a chance to speak with the captain and air their grievances. Similarly, you must abide by a code of mutual respect if you expect to establish secure and lasting love relationships. Thus, you can't try to cajole a person into thinking exactly like you and still expect them to feel close to you. If you are "on top" they, in effect, are below you and the relationship is no longer mutual. Secure attachment will not grow this way.

A related issue regarding not letting others define your reality is the idea you also don't have to stop doing what you need to do to take care of yourself just because someone else is mad at you. As stated previously, threats of violence are an exception and you clearly need to distance yourself from people who try to use excessive fear to control you. People who have been victimized and/or assume the role of caretaker are easily misaligned in response to another's anger. Anger implies rejection or harm to a caretaker and they tend to quickly give in. But they never feel safe; they never feel close in a secure way. This cannot be tolerated if you want secure love. To the contrary, the use of fear and expressions of excessive anger should be seen as signs of bullying. And bullying is a sign of fear and vulnerability in the other person. For example, when people get afraid and frustrated, instead of stating their needs to you, they get loud. If they stated their actual feelings they would be saying, "I'm threatened by you." "If I can't control you, I am scared I will be hurt." "You won't love me or take care of me." "You'll leave me if I don't force you to stay." "I don't feel safe in my love relationships, so I have to try to overpower you." People often mask their fears with anger. The key is to help them learn to translate their anger/fear into statements about their needs. We'll discuss more about how to do this shortly.

PROBLEM: People usually dislike it when others get mad at them.

SIMPLE SOLUTION 33: Remember, you don't have to stop doing what you need to do to take care of yourself, just because someone else is mad at you.

When it is Good to S.I.N.

A lot of people refuse to go to counseling and psychotherapy. While I believe in the necessity of mental health care, the reality of life is that people aren't immediately open to asking for help. Keep encouraging them though. There is a lot to be gained by going to a licensed professional for help. Sometimes people have to get to the point where their pain and the costs of not changing is greater than the social anxiety related to going to a professional. In the meantime, you might want to use a little S.I.N. to help lessen the intensity of conflicts.

S.I.N. is a tool for lessening people's emotional reactions and defensiveness during conflict. It stands for three things to say to a person whose feelings are overtaking them and they are starting to blame you or getting mad at you. There are a lot of reasons why S.I.N. works and I'll describe them as I outline its steps.

DIAGRAM 6: S.I.N.

S = "I'm **s**orry." (Then pause at least 5 seconds.)
I = "My **i**ntention was/is to...."
N = "I **n**eed....," or, "we **n**eed...."

The "**S**" stands for saying: "I'm sorry." That's all you say. Stop after you say this and pause. <u>Don't</u> add the word "but." Just say you are sorry and give these words a moment to sink in to their brain. Words can have a nice effect on brain chemistry. They are a major factor in many of the tools in this book for a good reason. Use them to make peace with your enemies and offer mutual respect. Also, do not say, "I am sorry," and then tag on the words, "That you feel that way." Saying either "but" or the latter phrase nullifies the good you want their brain to feel by hearing the words, "I'm sorry." Stop there. Let their brain absorb this short statement of repair.

Now, just because you say you are sorry does not mean you are responsible for their feelings or their difficulties. It is a statement of repair, to try and get mutual conflict solving back on track. The other person may have needed to hear someone say they are sorry forever, since childhood for example. You are not responsible for the depth and extent of others' feelings (unless you are blatantly abusing them) but you need to offer them some help if they are overtaken by strong feelings. Just say you are sorry and wait for a moment (a 5 second pause will suffice).

Next is "**I**" for your Intentions. Following S, you tell the person what your intention was or is. For example, you might say, "I didn't mean to hurt you. My intention was to get along better." Or, "My intention is to respect you. To care about you." Or, perhaps, "My intention is to regain your trust." There should be something positive communicated from you to the other person here. Your intentions matter. Furthermore, the "I" in S.I.N. is designed to show unity and mutualness. It shows the other person you are not just out for yourself, but you don't want the other person's needs to be more important than your own. It is a bridging statement and is very important for other people to hear, as you proceed to negotiate needs with them.

The "**N**" in S.I.N. represents a statement about your needs. It serves the purpose of not letting you fall into a caretaker's role and a position of victimization. You might say, "I need you to lower your voice." Or, "I need you to not call me names or threaten to leave me." You may also say things like, "I want you to listen to me too." And, "I need us to get along better." "I don't want the kids to be hurt by our arguing." "I want to find solutions to our problems we can both agree to." You get to decide on your need. The overarching goal is to establish mutual respect of needs. Your goal is neither to dominate nor be dominated.

Think of using S.I.N. like a fire extinguisher. It helps put out flame-ups during conflict triggered by the other's strong emotional reactions to you. It is especially useful for people with untreated or not fully resolved emotional problems from their childhood or other relationships. This applies to a lot of people. Someday more of the problems people have that are related to childhood abuse, neglect, or rejection will be treated more readily through mental health care and treated earlier in life, long before their marriages fail and other relationships suffer. Feelings related to past untreated childhood issues can be deceptive. People all too often blame others in the present for "causing" them to feel the way they do.

Emotional memories, especially traumatic and hurtful ones, last much longer than most people realize. People unfairly blame others for how they feel without any actual awareness about how their brain stores past information that inadvertently gets associated/triggered in current day relationships. Many a marriage or relationship has suffered due to this problem. Professional help is needed to resolve such problems. Until then, S.I.N. can help you navigate some difficult emotional moments during conflict with others.

PROBLEM: Important hurtful experiences from people's pasts don't easily go away with time.

SIMPLE SOLUTION 34: Emotional memories, especially traumatic and hurtful ones, last much longer than most people realize. Damaging hurtful experiences, including histories of being spoiled, require professional help to resolve. Use S.I.N. to help lessen the intensity of other's emotional reactions.

Other Thoughts about Emotional Land Mines and Feelings

You have to be careful managing conflicts with people who have untreated issues from their childhoods and past. Unknown emotional land mines exist for such people. You can find yourself asking, "What in the world just happened here?" as you witness the other person explode into an emotional melt-down. They may become outraged to the point of speaking homicidal accusations towards you. You may be dumbfounded about what you did that caused such a reaction. However, it is not necessarily you, but unseen meanings for the other person that your feelings, words, or actions trigger. People are often blamed for other people's feelings all too easily and falsely so. "You make me feel _____!" is a common statement in a lot of arguments. Or, people simply react negatively to one another without stopping to think about what else the current situation may be reminding them of that previously hurt or upset them. People are often all too sure that <u>you</u> are the cause of their feelings and problems. But given the emotional memory functions within each person's brain, this is very unlikely if not simply impossible.

The purpose of memory is to collect information from your life and use it for purposes of survival. The amygdala is one part of the emotional memory system in the brain that serves this purpose. By their very nature, memories are cumulative; memories are stored and later retrieved often automatically. Very hurtful experiences, in theory, create stronger and more lasting emotional memories that continue to affect current feelings and behavior long after the events happened. One could argue it is almost impossible to feel anything purely in the moment, due to how the brain encodes, stores, then applies information. No wonder meditation and various practices associated with philosophies like Buddhism try to help the person focus on living in the present moment and creating a relaxed state. Both are health-inducing practices likely to calm the person and aid them in being present and relaxed. It is always hoped such practices will have a lasting effect on the person. But even here, the more traumatized and deeply hurt people have been, the more likely they will be challenged by their memories of such events because that is simply how the creator designed our brains to work. Thus, we can seek solace and practice many valuable forms of relaxation and self-comfort, but our brains don't easily "forget" what happened to us. Such memories are stored in all those chemicals and circuits we have upstairs in our brains. Fortunately, language and compassion found in the hands of licensed mental health professionals or other caring and mature individuals can help shrink the residual effects of hurtful interpersonal or personal events and decrease the effects they have on our current day health and relationships.

PROBLEM: People will try and blame you alone for how they feel.

SIMPLE SOLUTION 35: Try to remember that people automatically (but falsely) assume that you are the cause of all their feelings and problems. Given the emotional memory functions within each person's brain, this is very unlikely if not impossible. And it seems people are always more able to see this in others than in themselves. Like singer Michael Jackson sang, "We have to stop and take a look at the man in the mirror." Thus, we must stop projecting our feelings onto others who "trigger" but don't necessarily cause the full intensity we feel them.

A couple common sayings associated with feelings are that, "No one makes you feel the way you do," and, "Feelings are not facts." To a great extent both are true. But the meanings events have for people can <u>trigger</u> an avalanche of hurt, anger, or outrage through our brain's emotional memory system, especially when people have unresolved hurts from other relationships. This is not to say that things like verbal, physical, sexual abuse and excessive neglect in childhood does not create very hurtful feelings by themselves. They undoubtedly do. Just like it immediately hurts to be in a car accident with physical injury, it also instantly hurts to experience physical, sexual and other abuses. Early childhood abuses can set the stage for a lifetime of relationships that recreate the harmful and hurtful patterns from our youth. Thus, feelings are often "triggered" when people have conflicts together and the more unaware each party is in their own unresolved life issues the less likely they will be to get along together and settle disputes in a reasonable mutually respectful way. Since it is assumed that most people do not seek out mental health counseling that would help them gain better self-understanding and lessen their emotional reactivity to others, in spite of obvious needs, this book is filled with tools to help address the outgrowth such problems create between people. All the tools are meant to support the overarching goal of mutual respect, which is the only way secure relationships (lasting love) can be created.

Another way to better understand exactly what feelings are is to consider them "artifacts." Artifacts are relics; they are made by a person with an association to one's past or subsequent use. And so it is with feelings. Feelings are the brain's neurological residue from past events. The more intense and important the past event was the more potent and strong the residue will be, as seen on the lasting effects feelings (and the meaning of events) have on current day reactions and behaviors.

PROBLEM: Sometimes our feelings can cripple us.

SIMPLE SOLUTION 36: Remember that feelings are neither facts nor fiction. But they matter greatly to us because they are "artifacts." That is, feelings are the neurological residue of the past significant events of our lives and the meanings we give them. Feelings have vital survival value for each of us. But we must be able to translate our feelings into specific needs and then communicate our needs first and foremost.

Now let's get back to emotional land mines and what to do about them. Let's first consider how talking or complaining about your feelings is one common way land mines in others can be triggered. Abuse victims and others who have been hurt through more serious rejection in life become very self-protective. The loss of love is not easily forgotten, especially if it occurs through trauma, betrayal, and blatant disrespect. A lot of times the ways and reasons people protect themselves are not obvious. As stated earlier in this book, self-protection in humans typically takes form in one of two ways: through either selfishness or excessive caretaking behaviors. In an off-handed way the selfish approach may be a little smarter (though ineffective in establishing lasting love). Selfishness indicates the person does not want to be a victim and taken advantage of (again?). In contrast, caretaking indicates the person is afraid of rejection and abandonment so they expend their energy pleasing others. Neither achieves secure love however; the selfish approach is only "better" if you think of the amount of energy each approach takes. Selfish people "enslave" caretakers and wear-out less quickly. Furthermore, extremes in selfishness and caretaking may indicate that an emotional land mine has either exploded or was nearly triggered. The words of caution I offer are: feeling statements may accidentally trigger feelings in the other person that are unresolved, especially if related to unfinished business from childhood or other relationships, and this can be very problematic or even dangerous. This is the nature of emotional land mines.

Stop and think about a time you told someone how you felt and they immediately responded with how they felt without any attention given to mutual needs or your need for solutions to your problems. Entering the "zone" of interpersonal feelings without needs statements leading the way can be risky business, especially with unseen emotional baggage in either party. Caution in this instance is applied through strategic tools of communication and conflict management strategies covered here. Hence, back-off from talking about your feelings when emotional pain is hemorrhaging. You should have been negotiating needs--yours' and theirs'--anyway. But, mistakes happen.

PROBLEM: Feeling statements by one person may accidentally trigger feelings in the other person that are unresolved, especially if related to unfinished business from childhood or other relationships, and this can be very problematic and worsen conflict.

SIMPLE SOLUTION 37: Learn to state your needs first before stating feelings. Be specific about what you need, first-and-foremost!

Sometimes, after mistakenly stepping on another's land mine, it causes an "explosion" in a relationship. Damage caused by exploding emotional mines can kill a relationship. Sometimes the damage is demonstrated by one spouse leaving the other or separating. Limbs to your life, in terms of your love relationships, can get blown off accidentally. At such moments there may not be anything another person can do to repair the harm done. In such cases, damage control is needed.

T.P.U. = Time, Patience, and Understanding

After a land mine explodes, relationship first aid might be initially limited to T.P.U.: Time, Patience, and Understanding. The person who feels extremely hurt may need time for their brain and entire nervous system to settle down, before talking further with you. Don't rush them. Trying to force someone back into a relationship with you prematurely, before they are ready to do so, after an emotional land mine has exploded, is like trying to force a soldier back into the field of battle before having a chance for their psyche to heal. It can simply make matters worse for both of you. You have to be patient. This can be hard to do when you face the loss of a primary love relationship in your life. You have to have a lot of understanding about what you did and, more importantly, what you triggered in your partner. If they do end their relationship with you, you are well-advised to review your relationship and conflict management knowledge and skills before restarting another relationship. People can only take so much love loss in their life without getting sick and falling apart.

PROBLEM: Emotional land mines exist for people who were hurt in past relationships but have not resolved their problems…a fact usually more obvious to others but not the person himself.

SIMPLE SOLUTION 38: After an emotional land mine explodes, and related hurt and tempers flare, relationship first aid is needed. Avoid throwing more feelings onto the emotional fire of an exploded reminder of a past hurt. Later, the focus needs to switch to needs clarification and use of S.I.N. and T.P.U.

When you do speak with the other person, be ready to listen to them. Don't start trying to direct their decision making. This can make matters worse. Inquire as to what they need. Try to get them to be specific about their needs as much as possible. Sometimes this is hard for them to do—T.P.U. is needed. If you haven't worked at valuing their needs before, you must do so now. But, you can never return to patterns of selfishness. I have seen situations where selfish people persist too long, maybe knowingly jumping up and down upon the other's land mine until finally succeeding in setting it off. An explosion occurs in their relationship, and their spouse decides to leave. Only then will the spouse left behind quickly learn to focus on meeting the other's needs. An attempt is desperately made to show interest in the other person returning to the relationship. However, history repeats itself since a "polarized brain" does not change easily or quickly. And the selfish person returns to previous patterns of relating. People only tolerate so many, "Here we go again," experiences before abandoning ship. You have to be fully committed to changing for good if you were previously caught up in selfish ways for the other person to regain trust and attach to you.

However, mutual respect is always the long-term goal. Only after the exploded partner is able to state some of their needs, and only after you have spent time meeting their needs, should you start to introduce your needs back into the relationship. Mutual respect of needs is imperative; there is no way a relationship can be secure if the needs of each person doesn't count. Temporary and exclusive focusing on the needs of others is sometimes necessary, such as in the case of emotional land mines. But, the balance in the relationship can't rest there. There must be mutual respect to achieve lasting love.

Conflict Math: Blame + Complain Does <u>Not</u> <u>Equal</u> Your Needs

This is a review of a conflict issue briefly discussed earlier. You should think in terms of basic mathematics for a moment. Also, consider the effects certain words have on others and the reactions those words elicit. Consider the words you use as affecting the other person's brain in such a way that they automatically react to you. Think in terms of "human relationship physics." Very simply, the acts of blaming and complaining to another person about their behavior do not equal specific communication about your needs. It seems to be a human reflex to automatically blame others and complain about problems. People think their needs are or should be obvious to another person. This is often not the case. Furthermore, blaming and complaining seem to automatically trigger defensiveness in the other person. It distracts them and you from clarifying exactly what mutual needs exist.

PROBLEM: The reflexive acts of blaming and complaining to another person about their behavior do not equal specific communication about your needs.

SIMPLE SOLUTION 39: Don't be fooled or waste precious time engaging in complaints or blame; make your specific needs known as soon as possible.

The moment someone starts to blame and complain about you, you should immediately ask them to specify their needs. There are several reasons for doing so. In addition to getting on track to have a more secure relationship with them through encouraging them to voice their needs, doing so also helps you stay out of the role of caretaker and victim. People sometimes use blame and complain to control others. Blame also gets the complainer out of taking responsibility for helping solve mutual problems. If you start to guess at their needs, you are taking ownership from them. Some relationships are entirely based on this dynamic. There is no secure intimacy associated with it. However, people who are afraid of love and closeness use these types of communication to control others and indirectly get their needs met. But, it is short-lived and ineffective in establishing secure love. A need people often have is to protect themselves from feeling anxiety and fear associated with mutual respect in their relationships. In effect, they fear love for some reason which is what gets created when mutual respect is part of a relationship. For example, people who are afraid to be vulnerable and intimate due to past family or relationship problems protect themselves from fear through blame and anger. This is another way selfishness (self-protection) arises in conflict and it must be redirected in a positive direction towards mutual respect.

You also have to be on the look out for hidden blame statements. For example, one way people blame others but conceal it in a "needs" statement is when they say: "I need you to understand..." This is a veiled attempt to communicate a need that actually is a hidden form for a complaint. Compelling a person to "understand" you also suggest the other's needs are irrelevant to you or their own reality counts less than your own. Statements like these actually indicate a desire for one-directional understanding and, therefore, they are controlling in nature. Such statements are sneaky ways to dominate others. Yet such statements are common as people are learning to move from general needs statements towards more specific ones. Thus, it is not enough to say you need something. You must be specific as to what your needs are and still be willing to respect the needs of the other person in return.

It is also important not to respond to blame or accusations with defensiveness. If you respond defensively, explaining why you did what you did, watch what happens. Defensiveness triggers more defensiveness; people almost can't help themselves. But no real problem solving occurs and if either party has a history of childhood abuse or rejection other hurt feelings are likely to be triggered. Conflicts can deepen and intensify without proceeding carefully. Don't respond to defensiveness with your own defensiveness. It is like emotional quicksand. Instead, get back on track as soon as possible. Ask the person what they are seeking and need. Thereafter, see if their needs can be met and introduce your needs to the negotiations as well. Your needs must count too.

PROBLEM: People often automatically rely on strategies of blaming and complaining. Conflicts between people only worsen when doing so.

SIMPLE SOLUTION 40: The moment someone starts to blame and complain about you, you should immediately get them to specify their needs. Or tell them "no." Then, state a need you have related to them immediately.

The Power of Questions

The person who asks the questions at any time in a conversation has the power. It helps to remember this when you are building relationships towards mutual respect. That is, use your power wisely. Let others share power with you, but don't let them dominate you by their questions. Your goal is mutual respect. Stop to think if it is in your interest to answer someone's question while in conflict with them. Ask yourself whether they are equally willing to answer your questions. If not, proceed carefully in your discussions with them. The more someone answers your questions with one of their own, the more they are disregarding your needs and seeking to control you. Similarly, the more people avoid answering your questions with techniques such as by trying to change the subject, the more careful you should be.

The give-and-take related to asking and answering questions is part of the learning process when trying to decrease selfishness and caretaking. Selfish people want to ask but not answer questions. Caretakers want to answer your questions to pacify and keep you at bay. It is another example how both directly and indirectly polarized people try to control each other. However, they engage in a dance of sorts that never produces lasting intimacy or love.

PROBLEM: People may use questions to badger or blame you. You'll notice they're not really interested in your answer. Instead, they just want a reaction. It gives them attention and a sense of control over you.

SIMPLE SOLUTION 41: Let others share power with you, but don't let them dominate you by their one-sided questions. For example, just because someone asks you a question doesn't mean you have to answer it especially when they aren't willing to answer questions when you ask them one.

Sometimes a Little L.S.D. Can Help

Since blaming is so prevalent in dysfunctional relationships, here is another tool you can use to try and stop its occurrence. L.S.D. stands for Label it, Stop it, and Direct it. It is a tool for trying to get problem solving back on track, once blame and complaining presents itself. In responding to such denunciations or accusations, the application of L.S.D goes like this. You first-**L**-Label what the person is doing. That is you verbally label what the accuser is doing, i.e., "You are blaming me." The second step-**S**-is to tell them, "Stop it." Next you want to redirect them toward communication about mutual needs. Thus, **D** is for Directing them to treat you differently. For example, "I don't want you to yell at me," or, better still, "Tell me what you need" (because you also will be telling them about your needs too). Label it, Stop it, and Direct it (L.S.D.) can together educate the other person about what they are doing and what you need them to do instead. It is another tool for making peace with your "enemy."

DIAGRAM 7: L.S.D.

L. Label what the other person is doing that you don't like.

S. Tell them to "stop it."

D. Direct them how you want to be treated instead.

Sprinkle on a Little Praise, it Helps, it Really Does

Professor Lupin, of the Harry Potter series, use to tell students while handing them a piece of chocolate, "Here, have a piece, it helps… it really does." He'd offer chocolate to them when they were hurt or distressed about something. So it is with praise and conflict management. If you are going through all the effort to align yourself with your needs and apply the variety of conflict tools and knowledge in this book, please remember to praise and reinforce others along the way. Tell others that you like it when they try to meet your needs. Also let them know how you appreciate them sharing their needs with you too. Praise them for their effort and interest. Sometimes you have to encourage them with statements like, "You can do it," or, "I know it's hard, thanks for trying." Encourage others not give up, when you see them making efforts but struggling to learn new ways of relating.

Sometimes it seems people are afraid to compliment or thank people for changing their ways. Fears related to intimacy and having secure love are concealed in various forms. Being reluctant to encourage or praise your partner is one of them. Yet, interpersonal praise is very powerful and can help shorten the struggle to achieve mutual respect if it is sprinkled into communications around conflict. Thus, be brave and if you want somebody to keep trying to respect your needs reinforce them by thanking them for their effort. Both of you have something to gain, with secure love being strengthened.

PROBLEM: It is easy to overlook others' attempts to treat you differently.

SIMPLE SOLUTION 42: Tell others that you like it when they try to meet your needs. Also let them know how you appreciate them sharing their needs with you too.

Chapter 8

THE IMPORTANCE
OF FEELINGS

The Feelings Funnel

With so much emphasis thus far about voicing the needs that arise from your feelings, it will be helpful if you have additional information about feelings and how they are related to conflict management. Let's take a look at Diagram 8, the Feelings Funnel. The Feelings Funnel is the model I will use to discuss feelings and their relationship to resolving conflicts with people.

First, it helps if you understand that feelings are biological in nature. Within each person's brain is circuitry that processes and stores emotional memories. Some areas of the brain that handle these memories include the amygdala, hippocampus, and associated regions. The brain reacts differently to events having highly charged emotional meaning. For our purposes, all life experiences have varying degrees of emotional value, with some having more emotional significance than others. Thus, at the top of the funnel is a large opening. Consider it a pool or reservoir of collected life events and their relative emotional importance. Some events were good, some bad, and some fairly neutral in terms of emotional relevance to you. The respective emotional "meanings" of all events are biologically encoded in the brain and stored there. You aren't aware this is going on, but it happens. Functional Magnetic Resonance Imaging has helped map such occurrences. Your brain is similar to search engines on the internet that "remember" your past interests and search topics. It encodes things and stores them for future use. Your brain "remembers" what happened to you, regardless of whether your conscious mind chooses to or not. That is, just because you may deny or ignore the significance of past emotionally important events your brain and body don't necessarily like it when you do. Symptoms, both physical and psychological, can arise indicating that other problems exist that you may not be ready for, or want to, address. That's partially why there is so much emphasis on paying attention to your feelings in most areas of mental health care and, to some extent, physical health treatment. But there are problems related to only paying attention to your feelings.

Towards the lower portion of the Feelings Funnel is a square that encompasses a "recent event." This is where things get more interesting—where conflict management becomes challenging. As you live your life today, current events will *trigger* a feeling or feelings. One of the biggest mistakes people make with each other when dealing with conflict is to falsely assume that what they are feeling in the present moment is directly caused by the current event. So many arguments between people are magnified and worsened when people "miss-assume" that the full extent of their anger or frustration is caused by the other person right now. Based on how the brain stores information, I would suggest that is impossible. Your brain reacts out of its rich and extensive history of encoded life events since you were born. This is where the idea of "overreacting" arises. Other people can more easily see how we overreact to certain life events, better than we can. It's humbling. None of us are as good as we think we are in terms of knowing ourselves and exactly why our brains fire-off feelings of the intensity they do. So one thing we all must do is to stop assuming that other people cause the full extent of what we are feeling. It just isn't so. Thus, our current relationships become more complicated when strong emotional memories get triggered by current life events.

PROBLEM: People are too quick to blame others for how they feel.

SIMPLE SOLUTION 43: One thing we all must do is to stop assuming that people cause the full extent of what we are feeling. Work to improve self-awareness about how past events affect present feelings, if you want to reduce the chances of over reacting to others in the present.

Next, I must reemphasize that feelings matter. They matter a lot. They are in essence our brain's message to us that what is going on presently is triggering some important aspect of our personal history and may have vital survival value. The more intense our feelings, especially when they are of the negative variety like anger, fear, or sadness, the more relevant they are to our lives and the people we associate with.

Now, I hope the reasoning behind Materna's Law #1 makes more sense. No matter what feelings you are stuck with, it is better to proceed with statements about needs because your needs help settle your feelings. The venting of your emotions alone is less likely to achieve the settling of feelings compared to needs. In essence, your needs are your solutions, if not permanently then at least temporarily. However, you have to be careful. Due to the cumulative effect of emotional memories stored in your brain, it can be easy to overreact to how you feel. Some people prematurely decide they need to end a relationship based on a momentary, but intense, feeling. Sometimes such extreme solutions might not be necessary. Singer Jimmy Buffet has a song about tattoos. He refers to them as a, "Permanent reminder of a temporary feeling." Similarly, you have to be careful what you demand of others or impose upon them regarding your needs. Sometimes people prematurely decide to end a relationship based on their current strong feelings, not realizing those feelings actually are in response to a previous life experience. Thus, you also need to be careful about your needs, to some extent, and act in measured ways.

PROBLEM: People can overreact to present day stressors when unsettled problems from their past erupt intensely in the present. Some people prematurely decide they need to end a relationship based on a momentary, but intense, feeling.

SIMPLE SOLUTION 44: Due to the cumulative effect of emotional memories stored in your brain, it can be easy to overreact to how you feel. Try and act in measured ways and avoid extreme solutions if you can.

If stating your current needs is ineffective or not practical to resolve your feelings, then your feelings may need help--to "shrink" them down a bit. This is where psychotherapy or counseling is useful. If your feelings are so overpowering and negatively affect your ability to cope, they are preventing you from identifying realistic needs in the present and you are well-advised to seek professional help. It is just like with cancer. If you have cancer cells and risk them spreading throughout your body, your life can depend on ridding your body of those cells. So it is with highly charged emotional events from your past. Take care of them before they sicken you and your relationships. Avoid unnecessary losses in love relationships whenever you can!

DIAGRAM 8: FEELINGS FUNNEL

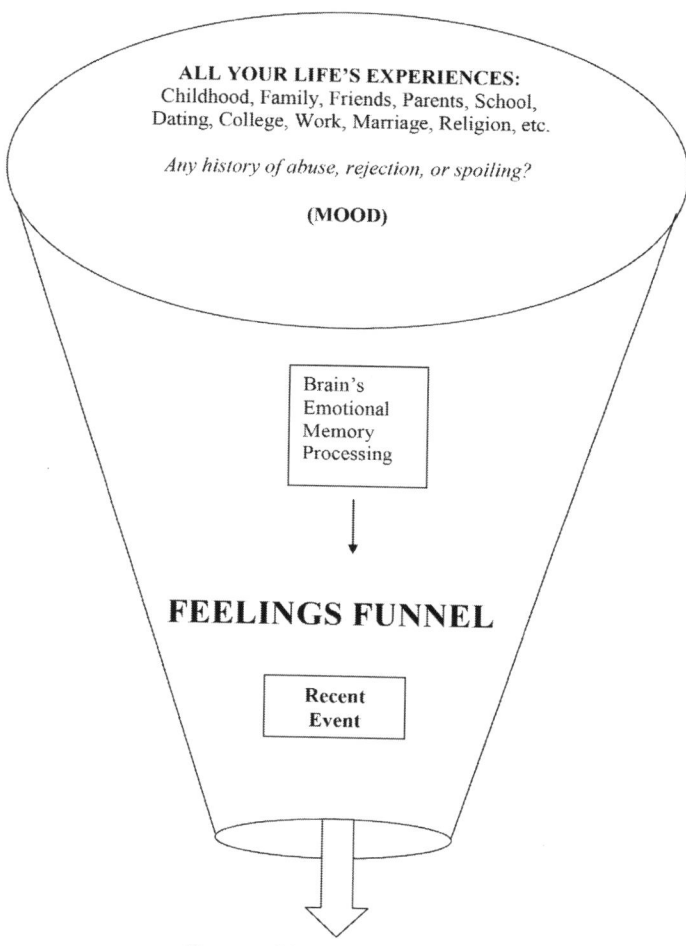

ALL YOUR LIFE'S EXPERIENCES:
Childhood, Family, Friends, Parents, School,
Dating, College, Work, Marriage, Religion, etc.

Any history of abuse, rejection, or spoiling?

(MOOD)

Brain's
Emotional
Memory
Processing

FEELINGS FUNNEL

**Recent
Event**

Current Moment's Feeling

The Difference Between a Mood and a Feeling

What's the difference between a mood and a feeling? The difference makes a difference when it comes to conflict management and the application of needs. According to Wikipedia.com, a mood is a relatively long lasting emotional state. Moods differ from feelings in that they are less specific, less intense, and less likely to be triggered by a particular event. Moods generally have either a positive or negative quality; people speak of being in a good mood or a bad mood. In contrast, feelings are more acute and shorter lasting. Feelings are often triggered by current day events. Moods are generally expansive and affect a person in a broader manner. Feelings are of shorter duration. However, feelings can become more expansive and have far-reaching effects on your life if you let them, that is, if you fail to translate them into your needs. For example, if you don't deal with your feelings and related needs in a timely fashion, things can get backed-up for you psychologically and emotionally resulting in a worsening of mood. So it may be for the "grumpy old man" syndrome; if people's feelings and needs are not responded to in mutually respectful ways, people's love relationships suffer. As people get older, if they become more bitter and alone, it may be because the issue of mutual respect was never established in their relationships with others and their attachment to others was too weak to sustain contact. In contrast, people who apply mutual respect are more likely to have love in their lives until the very end.

If you refer back to the Feelings Funnel (Diagram 8) you will see that mood is placed at the top of the funnel. Moods can represent a sense of entrapment. That is, a mood can be conceived of as the reflections in your brain regarding the range of experiences you've had in your life and the net emotional effects. Being stuck in "mood-land" is no fun. It's what all the antidepressant commercials on television portray; people stuck in their moods need a way out. They feel trapped and anchored in their mood. But what else can you do to change your mood?

A Code of Conduct

Moods such as irritability, hopelessness, hyperactivity, and chronic worry sometimes need medication to help govern them. Having a mood disorder is a big deal in terms of mental health care, but it is treatable. Another intervention for mood problems is to have a code of conduct for yourself. A code of conduct is a thought-based intervention on your behalf that you live by. One example is the Ten Commandments. It is a set of guidelines people are supposed to follow, regardless of mood and the life situations they find themselves in. God and other authors of the Bible must have realized this a long time ago. Similarly, Crosby Stills, Nash and Young had a song, *Teach your Children*, that went, "You, who are on the road, must have a code that you can live by." Thus, another form of mood management is to have a set of guidelines or a code of conduct you follow in your life to manage or protect yourself from the negative effects of your mood. (See Appendices I & II for Codes of Conduct (Commandments) for caretakers and overly "self-preserving" people.)

PROBLEM: People can get lost and confused in their intense moods and feelings resulting in cruel and hostile treatment of others.

SIMPLE SOLUTION 45: Another form of mood management is to have a set of guidelines or a code of conduct for you to follow in your life to manage or protect yourself from the negative effects of your mood.

Codes for conduct can be identified for a range of common problems. For example, people often drink alcohol, do drugs, eat excessively, or participate in other compulsive behaviors to manage their moods. When choices are made to only sedate symptoms of negative moods, deterioration in functioning is likely. Treatment programs for addictions include codes of conduct. They help define what you should and shouldn't do, no matter what your mood is. Alcoholics Anonymous' concept of "stinking thinking" is an example of a negative mood indicator and thoughts which are to be avoided and countered with healthier ones, in order to avoid relapsing. People who eat or drink excessively, in response to their mood, need their own codes of conduct that define other ways to manage moods. Following a diet can be seen as a type of code. It guides people regarding their behaviors no matter what mood they are in. So is the code of not going grocery shopping when you are hungry. In addition, how often have you heard people say, when planning a meal, "What am I in the mood to have tonight?" The same thing can be said for choosing the type of alcohol consumed. People's moods can carelessly direct their choices. Codes of conduct are needed in life. Parents should take steps to "teach their children well" regarding codes of conduct to best prepare them for the future. Even our highway and traffic laws can be viewed as socially sanctioned codes of conduct. We don't want people driving at speeds based on their mood. What a disaster that would be!

Another way to alter your moods over time is to learn to act on your needs in response to your feelings. It really sounds like paying attention to your needs, related to your feelings, and applying them in life is the answer to all your problems. Yes, I think that conceptually this is true. Since secure love is based on the mutual respect of needs, the benefits of mutually respectful relationships is undeniable.

If you look at the Feelings Funnel again (Diagram 8), you can see that the feelings you have in any moment are in fact related to your general mood. What you want to be able to do is not let there be a backup of sorts within the funnel. That is, the more you translate your feelings into your needs the more "flow" there is through the funnel. In contrast, blocking or denying your feelings and detaching yourself from your needs can create an impaction of sorts. A back up occurs whereby your brain reflects more of your mood state. People don't do well if they operate out of negative mood states. Thus, you can also modify your mood over time by honoring your feelings and related needs. The relief your brain feels will be welcomed by it; constipation of any type is generally uncomfortable. But remember, start with speaking of your needs and not your feelings. It is safer for you. You'll also decrease the amount of conflict blockage you experience.

Chapter 9

CONFLICT SOLUTIONS MODEL

A 4 Stage Model for Settling Conflicts with Mutual Respect

Now that we have covered a range of issues and tools for resolving conflicts with others, let's discuss a model or framework for applying them. This conflict resolution model is divided into four steps:

STEP ONE: Identifying your own ideas and feelings. Related questions to ask yourself in Step One are: What are you uncomfortable with? What is bothering you? What do the other person's actions trigger in you? What meaning do their actions have for you?

STEP TWO: Translate your ideas and feelings into statements about your needs. Both groups of needs must count: yours and the other person's.

STEP THREE: Concentrate on joining your needs with those of the other person's. Each person's needs are their proposed solutions to their problems or concerns. Both parties must agree to the mutual importance of each individual's needs.

STEP FOUR: Think about compromises, taking turns, or making exchanges on one need for another. In step four each person works to agree on how both parties needs can get met to some degree. They also agree about what exchanges might be necessary where one person does something in trade for the other person doing something for them. Fairness and mutual respect are key components throughout the conflict resolution process. Now let's consider each stage of the model in more depth.

Step One: Ideas and Feelings

You have to start somewhere if you want to solve a problem. People typically are of one of two types. One type considers a problem in regards to his or her thoughts and ideas about it. The second type is guided primarily by their feelings. Of course in many cases people blend both thoughts and feelings together, but as a general guideline people are typically dominated by either their thoughts or feelings with each being an important source of information. Thus, each person has a way of identifying within themselves that a problem exists. Once a problem is recognized based on how you feel or what you think what do you do next? Or what shouldn't you do next?

What you shouldn't do is discolor your feelings by using your thoughts to minimize them or discredit them. For example, don't say to your self, "I shouldn't feel this way." In other words don't use your thoughts to talk your self out of how you really feel. You won't be able to accurately represent your true needs in resolving conflicts if you do. Your goal is to just simply accept how you feel without judging yourself or launching into a blaming session with the other person about how they "make" you feel.

Step Two: Individual Needs and Intentions

So far I have emphasized the importance of translating feelings into needs without giving additional importance to the thoughts people have that modify or translate feelings into needs. In addition, some people insist that your thoughts determine your feelings and if you think differently you will feel differently. While thoughts certainly can modify feelings, and need to sometimes, I have found that only relying on thoughts or rationalizations to modify feelings and therefore your needs can indirectly support a sense of victimization and caretaking. If you color over your true feelings too much, your needs won't be accurately aligned with your feelings and your problems are likely to persist. You can repeat thoughts or rationalizations over and over, but if your needs aren't getting met you will be less likely to achieve secure attachments in life. Thinking your way out of your feelings can be problematic in terms of producing a hidden source for victimization. If you deny your feelings and needs, and others in life are doing similarly, you are adding insult to injury. Since this book is intended to limit peoples' attraction to caretaking or selfish roles in relationships I will not emphasize the importance of rationale thoughts by themselves. In contrast I will include thoughts that support your path toward establishing mutually respectful relationships.

An intervening factor between Step One and Step Two is to define for yourself (think about) what your true intentions are as you use your feelings to pinpoint your needs. Is your intention to dominate the other party? Is it to solely save face or defend your position? Is it to attack the other person or "put them in their place?" If it is any of these you will not be successful in establishing a mutually respectful relationship. Some people think they want respectful and lasting relationships with others, but they don't act that way. In addition, some people are so defended they either can't or don't care about the needs of others; their sole purpose is to dominate them. In order to be successful, your intention must be to assert your needs <u>and</u> value the needs of the other person. Anything short of this will not produce lasting love and attachment.

Also in Step Two, listening to each other is critical. Listening and showing our care are pivotal when practicing mutual respect. It calls to mind age old Biblical wisdom to, "be fast to listen, slow to speak, and even slower to anger." In a related fashion, if fear is anchoring you in terms of how you approach relationships, you are less likely to listen, less likely to show respect, more likely to misperceive the other and derail the conflict resolution/relationship building process by trying to exert control over it. There can be lots of love in your heart (you mean well), but fear can overpower the love and interfere with your attempts to get along with others. So, take care to lessen your fears as discussed earlier – it is essential. Learn to stop and listen to each other and show that you are listening by repeating out loud what the other person is saying to you.

Step Three: Couple/Relationship Oriented Solutions

As you progress from the second to third stage of conflict resolution, after voicing your needs and hearing the others', you each propose solutions. Again, if listening is not occurring, conflict resolution gets derailed and reaching simple solutions to your problems is hampered. You must be able to listen to the other person and show them you hear their position. You don't have to agree with them, but you do have to demonstrate that you hear them and value their position, needs, and ideas. Learn to paraphrase, that is, repeat or summarize what you hear them saying, to show respect through listening. The solutions you propose should reflect the combined needs in your relationship. Basically your needs lead you to your solutions but cooperation between both parties is required. Mutual respect is needed here to formulate real solutions and to counter the tendencies to be either too self-serving or other-serving. Again, selfishness or caretaking never creates a mutually respectful lasting relationship by themselves.

PROBLEM: People often don't feel heard or respected in conversations and this can trigger emotional land mines.

SIMPLE SOLUTION 46: Learn to paraphrase (summarize) what the other person is saying. You can simply tell them, "So what I hear you saying is...." Then wait to see if you heard them right. Using check-in statements like, "Do you feel I am respecting your needs?" or, "Do you feel like I am hearing you correctly?" can also help. Afterwards, be sure they also stop and show you similar respect and paraphrasing. Turn-taking is essential.

Immediately, after a person's ideas and feelings are identified and needs are expressed, intentions are communicated either directly or indirectly. For example, a person may directly tell you, "I want to work this out and get along better with you." Or, indirectly, a kind and patient voice tone implies desire to work problems out with respect. Conversely, people can voice demands, get angry, start to yell or scream, call names, ask a bunch of questions, and stop listening to you. Disrespect may quickly arise during conflicts with some people. If the intentions are based on mutual respect/love and not hampered by fear/over control, the chances for simple solutions to life problems is more likely. Again, fear and its various forms of dominance and control immediately counter simple direct problem solving. Fears typically prevent healthier forms of relating and need to be addressed and decreased. As we'll discuss in the next chapter, caretakers in relationships with narcissistic people require additional unique tools and strategies. This is due to the fact that both parties have specific fears that need to be countered through strategic communication and specialized conflict skills.

PROBLEM: People's fight-or-flight response can over-take them and trick them into over responding in a dominating fashion.

SIMPLE SOLUTION 47: If people's intentions are based on mutual respect/love and not hampered by fear/over control, the chances for simple solutions to life problems is more likely. Think mutual; both people's needs must be considered.

Step Four: Compromise

After solutions are proposed by both parties, the fourth stage is to seek compromises. In a compromise neither person totally gets their way; neither person may be totally happy with the proposed compromise. That is, unless the goal is mutual respect a compromise might not actually be viewed as a successful end state. Compromises are inherently needed so that neither party is violated with regards to respect of their needs. Similarly, taking turns is another form of compromising. Furthermore, it could be said that, "If you truly love someone, compromise with them." That way, it is less likely you'll have to "set them free."

Here's an example of a dysfunctional conflict discussion between a caretaker and her selfish partner (A). The first example is followed by an application of the 4 Stage Conflict Model (B):

EXAMPLE A:

Cathy Caretaker: "I was wondering if it would be OK with you if we visited my mother? We haven't seen her in a year."

Nate Narcissist: "Your mother? Why do you always want to go see her? You're such a baby!"

Cathy Caretaker: "OK. I was just wondering…"

Nate Narcissist: "Let's go see my mother instead. She's nicer to me."

Cathy Caretaker: "OK, if you want to."

EXAMPLE B:

Mary Mutual: "Would it be OK with you if we stopped by my mom's house on the way home? (Feeling: Mary is worried about her mom who has been ill. Need: To check-in on mother.) I haven't seen her in a while. I am worried about her cough. I was going to take her some soup."

Mike Mutual: "I was thinking we could stop by my brother's on the way home tomorrow." I wanted to help him, like I promised. (Feeling: Mike was concerned about his brother's taxes having to be filed to avoid a penalty. Need: To keep his promise.)

Mary Mutual: "Could we do both?" (Their intention is for both needs to count. They start to discuss solutions.)

Mike Mutual: "Possibly. What do you suggest?"

Mary Mutual: "What if we drop off the soup and visit her for an hour. Afterwards we can stop at your brother's."

Mike Mutual: "No, my brother is going out of town at 1:00. Can we stop at his house first, then your mother's?" (Compromise is necessary.)

Mary Mutual: "OK. That should work for us."

Mike Mutual: "Thanks." (Mutual respect is reinforced.)

Other Points about the Four Stage Conflict Model

A few other points need to be reemphasized about this model. Stage 2 and 3 are related. Your needs are your solutions to your problems, feelings, and related ideas. If both people have the same needs, and they get met, conflict is over. Conflict is usually a bit more challenging than that, however, and conflicting needs take a bit more effort to resolve. Each party needs to persist, because their needs are tied to all that (hopefully) matters to them: a need for secure love. This is another reason it is better to befriend or marry someone similar to you, as social psychology research has shown in the past. Your needs will conflict less if you share more things in common with your partner.

In looking at the model of conflict resolution presented in this chapter and thinking about the issue of conflicting needs, you might think that people are frequently prone to stalemates where neither is willing to budge from their position and respective needs. When mutual respect is a regular part of the dialogue and a primary part of a relationship, stalemates are rare. I associate the reasons for this to human physics and brain chemistry. There is something appreciated and welcomed by the human brain when it recognizes that people are willing to share and take turns meeting needs. The brain seems to retain and store this information and is able to tolerate its needs sometimes not counting, at least temporarily. Stalemates and outright rejection of others' needs is more common when selfishness and narcissistic brains are in play. Brains infected by selfishness don't do well with compromise, but don't give up total hope. There are some things to try first, as described throughout this book.

Another element critical to healthy problem solving and achieving simple solutions is the concept of "exchanges." Exchanges are placed between stages 3 and 4. The idea of exchanges is that both parties' needs must count and over time there needs to be a pattern of fairness and equality built into the relationship. That is, each person's needs get met in specific ways, at times, in exchange for the willingness to support the other person getting their needs met in specific ways at a later time. Basically, exchanges represent the reappearance of the Golden Rule and mutual respect of needs. You have to be willing to take turns. You also have to be able to trust that your needs will count too. Similarly, fears associated with meeting other's needs must be contained if not eradicated. A selfish person's brain must be prepared to better accept the process of taking turns, since it is a fundamental part of building lasting love relationships. In fact, fear is at the heart of problems for narcissists <u>and</u> caretakers. We will discuss novel ways of managing such fears in the next chapter.

Chapter 10

RELATING WITH PEOPLE WHO HAVE "SELFISH-BRAIN DISEASE"

Selfish-Brain Disease

In March 2011, I was listening to a morning news show on the radio. There was a report from an eye witness of the devastating earthquake and tsunami in Japan that had just occurred. After he described the fear and chaos associated with the earthquake, he explained how the people in Japan opened their doors to others in need of comfort and shelter. One example was how a hotel opened its lobby to displaced passer-byes and put out chairs so people could sit and rest. There were other reports of people doing the same thing in their homes. That is, assuming their homes were still standing. Then the radio announcer compared the Japanese response with what might happen in the U.S.A. He complained, "It's not like it is here, where people would shut their doors in your face." It sometimes appears that many in the U.S.A. have a selfish outlook on life. Whether "Selfish Brain Disease" is of pandemic proportion or not is hard to determine, but it is a common component in many relationship problems. Everyone deserves a better understanding of it and would benefit from information on how to modify its impact. That is, Selfish Brain Disease is a common source of much human suffering. Everyone needs to know what to do when it presents itself and tries to take root in your life.

In this chapter I will be teaching you to quickly identify excessively selfish people, typically referred to as narcissists. However, I will not belabor the attention given to descriptions of narcissists; they likely get too much of your attention already! Instead, I will emphasize tools to use in your relationships with narcissists and others having selfish dispositions that are aimed at <u>strengthening</u> attachment and secure love. Even though there are no magic cures found here, the principles and tools I describe for you are unique and have shown promise in my professional work with others struggling to maintain relationships with narcissists. The tools go beyond just asserting yourself and setting boundaries. That is, assertiveness and setting boundaries are necessary skills when relating to narcissists, but by themselves are insufficient if your goal is to shape a more secure love relationship. Again, the major idea for you to focus on is that mutual respect of needs is the only way to establish secure love and narcissists are no exception. Direct approaches like insisting on your needs counting don't work well by themselves. Tools that include joining and shared values must be applied if the narcissist, as well as yourself, is ever to develop beyond the "me-versus-you" battle triggered by assertiveness alone. Remember, even though you must be able to define and voice your needs, to establish lasting love and intimacy your goal must also focus on the establishment of mutual respect.

PROBLEM: Being assertive by itself is not enough to join in a collaborative relationship with someone who tends to be selfish in nature.

SIMPLE SOLUTION 49: Tools that include joining and shared values must be applied if the narcissist, as well as yourself, is ever to develop beyond the "me-versus-you" battle triggered by assertiveness alone.

A Quick Glimpse at Selfish People

What are some easy ways to identify selfish/narcissistic people? Let's think about the ways in which they relate to you. For example, narcissists are people who only want to talk about themselves. They only want to do what is in <u>their</u> best interest without considering the effects of their behaviors on others. They <u>act</u> as if they are the only person in the room with a valid opinion or an idea worth considering. They scoff at others' points of view and are quick to discount your input. They display a grandiose air of importance and want you to get on board <u>their</u> train. They are overly concerned about how they appear to others, often giving extra care to their physical appearance and feeling angry if their ideas are publicly challenged. If you confront them, they'll either react with blame or criticism or abruptly walk away in anger. Sometimes they'll indirectly draw attention to themselves saying, "I can't do anything right!" They structure communication and relationships as if setting up a perimeter on a battle field. But, what are they defending against? They talk over you and interrupt your speech. They (try to) limit you, to address <u>their</u> needs, admire <u>their</u> ideas, and follow <u>their</u> lead. It is no wonder so many narcissistic people end up working in positions of power and authority. They need to be in control of others. But why is this? What are they trying to preserve? What are they afraid of?

Narcissists:
- Only want to talk about themselves
- Only want to do what is in their best interest
- Disregard how they affect others
- Act like their opinion is the only valid one
- Discount others' opinion if different than their own
- Dole-out blame and criticism reflexively
- Draw attention to themselves directly and indirectly through complaints
- Mistakenly believe that love is based on how much attention they get
- When they complain they want you to rescue them and guess their needs <u>without</u> them telling you what they are
- Make statements or comments but without finishing them, wanting you to do the work of reading their minds

Let's think about narcissist's behaviors and contrast them with what a "healthy" person might do. Someone able and willing to relate with mutual respect would acknowledge you. They'd greet you when meeting you and say hello. Maybe they would ask, "How are you?" They'd acknowledge your presence. They would introduce you to others and include you, not exclude you, in conversations. If they disagreed with you, they would do so without attack and rejection of your ideas. You wouldn't get the sense that the world has to function only as they see it. They would allow you to have your own opinion and ideas. Thus, the need to control others would not be the overarching rule in interpersonal transactions.

There's an old saying that goes, "The more in control someone needs to be, the more out of control their lives were in the past." If we assume this is true for narcissists, then in what ways were their lives out of their control? Their underlying fear had to come from somewhere. As stated earlier in this book, narcissists' need to control others and their related fears can come from rejection, being excessively discounted in life (by another narcissist, perhaps a parent), or through being spoiled. Early losses such as of a parent through death or divorce may leave a person equally vulnerable. Sometimes narcissists were sickly as children, and the extra care they needed taught them that their needs counted more than others. No matter the reason for being discounted, rejected or spoiled narcissists or others saw the need to cater to them. Narcissists are usually treated, or act like, they are royalty and others should serve them. Their excessive self focus has survival value for them. It is their attempt to maintain love relationships, as faulty as the outcome is. Unidirectional needs never produce secure love, such as what occurs in narcissism and caretaking. Only mutual respect gives rise to lasting intimacy. But why do narcissists persist at only wanting their needs to be met?

At the top of a narcissist's problems, which may or may not be in their awareness, is their belief that there is a very limited supply of attention and love in their world and they better grab all they can before it is gone. <u>Seeking attention is equivalent to being loved for narcissists.</u> If the love around them is not secure, and such insecurity can be in the form of a lack of attention or a flooding of it, give-and-take has not been part of their life and they are desperate to get their needs met. "Look at me," they might say or act in a like fashion. Some people get this way when raised as an only child. Having siblings may help people learn to be more mutually respectful, but it is no guarantee. Some narcissists focus excessively on their dress. They seek attention through an impeccable physical appearance; they helplessly crave the glance of others to reassure them they are valued. "Aren't I pretty?" or, "Aren't I handsome?" they seem to be saying to others. "Aren't I smart?" "Don't I have great ideas?" They are desperate to know that they matter to you, even more than you do.

PROBLEM: Seeking attention is <u>equivalent to</u> being loved for narcissists. They want others to give them attention or get out of their way so that they can glean attention from others. They are starving to feel loved. But attention, by itself, will never meet their insatiable needs.

SIMPLE SOLUTION 50: Narcissists must learn that there is no security for them in solely seeking attention. Most can come to recognize failed relationship histories. Some go on to recognize that they never knew what the nature of their relationship failures were. Others are both surprised and grateful to pinpoint what has been going wrong in their lives and decide to work on changing outcomes.

Narcissists: -Act as if there is a very limited supply of attention and love in the world
-Seek any attention they can get
-Believe that getting attention is equal to being loved
-Are desperate to know they matter to you, even more than you do

Dramatic and public displays of anger are not uncommon either, since they always find ways to draw attention to themselves physically, emotionally, or through their ideas. If your attention isn't quickly forthcoming, they have no need for you and will seek to find another person to reflect their value back to them. And by the way, if it is not already obvious, narcissists won't like it when you ignore them. When you trigger their narcissistic soft spot of feeling vulnerable in the area of secure love, through any self-perceived loss of attention, unlovable and hurt they will feel. They will then reflexively blame you for how they feel. Get ready to be rejected or attacked in some fashion. They are very sensitive creatures, but would never admit it.

You might also wonder if anyone ever stopped and tried to teach a narcissist how to share attention with others? But even if someone tried to teach them to share, narcissists' desperate need for attention is the result of a deep lack of security. All narcissists are historically vulnerable due to not having secure attachments with others, where their (and others') needs counted. And those insecure feelings were related to being insecurely loved by significant others, most often their parents. There is no security in being spoiled either; spoiled kids learn that only their needs count. When others reject or avoid spoiled children for not being good playmates their only recourse is to draw more attention to themselves. They learn to relate unidirectionally, not mutually. Rejection only triggers more of the same self-centered relating. They want someone to meet their needs, and only their needs. Give-and-take is not in their repertoire (yet).

Nobody Wants to Be a Victim

A story from my past illustrates another point. When I was in graduate school, I was having a conversation with a professor about narcissistic people. I was complaining to him about a narcissistic person I was having trouble with. I was both surprised and angered when he said to me, "You know, narcissists need love too." That was how our conversation ended. Boy did his comment annoy me. I came to him for understanding and support. Now, he was telling me about the narcissist's need for attention and love. I then wondered about his credibility. "What a narcissistic response," I groveled. But that was over 20 years ago and I never forgot his comment. They (narcissists) need love too. Now I realize he was right. They just don't know how to get their needs met without dominating others. So if there is to be some sense of a "cure" for narcissism in relationships it is likely to only be achieved by one basic fact of life: everybody needs love. Narcissists may say they don't need or value feelings including love, but they are wrong or, should I say, in a heck of a lot of denial. The real challenge is in devising methods to lessen narcissists' fears and anxiety just enough where they still feel some control over their relationship yet are willing to consider the needs of others. The only way they and others can achieve secure love is through mutual respect of needs. Anything less will fail. Thus, conversations with narcissists <u>must</u> include mutually respectful language and communication.

PROBLEM: Narcissists are very vulnerable people. However, they are the last to recognize it and go to great lengths to deny it. It seems as if their brains get polarized in regards to how they look at getting personal needs met. They fight for their needs to count, solely and primarily.

SIMPLE SOLUTION 51: The real challenge is in devising methods to lessen narcissists' fears and anxiety about being hurt or rejected again, just enough where they still feel some control over their relationship yet are willing to consider the needs of others. Narcissists need love too but they need help realizing it and then learning how to take turns with others.

Chapter 11

THE POLARITY OF MIND
REFLEX REVISTED

A Review

The Polarity of Mind Reflex was first introduced in Chapter 2. I want to review it here and then further describe ways to counteract the negative affect our fight-or-flight response has on intimate relationships, friendships, and love.

DIAGRAM 9: THE POLARITY OF MIND REFLEX

STEP 1: You experience rejection, abandonment, abuse, or spoiling. Or you simply have never been taught how to create mutual respect in relationships.

STEP 2: You must survive; children rely on adults for safety, caring, and nurturance.

STEP 3: If parents don't meet your needs for security, how will you get them met? (Spoiling or doting on children never aids them in terms of future relationship security.)

STEP 4: Your brain automatically directs you toward two groups of behaviors: A. You focus on others' needs or, B. You strictly focus on your needs getting met. This is the Polarity.

STEP 5: <u>Mutual</u> respect of needs in relationships is not learned and applied.

STEP 6: Secure love and attachment is prevented.

STEP 7: You never experience secure and lasting love. People don't attach well to you because you are unable to practice mutual respect of needs. People leave you or you leave them, because love and attachment doesn't get established. You wonder why you have to either cope with repeated losses or live your life never truly feeling loved.

Now even though the Polarity of Ming Reflex is not based on scientific brain analysis like CAT scans or MRIs, it is based on my studies, experiences, and work as a clinical psychologist and marital therapist. It is also based on commonly held beliefs about our brains. Our brain's primary purpose is to oversee our survival. Similarly, our fight-or-flight system within our brains uses emotional risk information from our environments to guide us to safety. Thus, whether we are concerned about actual physical threats to our lives or anxiety related sensations associated with our attachments to others, our fight-or-flight responses guide our actions. Some of these "actions" pertain to our words and the way we voice our needs in our most important relationships. Our needs communicate what each of us need in regards to our survival. But the polarity of our fight-or-flight reactions causes us to seek to dominate others or shrink from asserting our own needs. Secure attachment will never be achieved if we allow our basic fight-or-flight instincts to dominate us in this way.

Caretaking as Flight From Your Needs

Let's review caretaking behaviors. Caretaking is designed to show others we are of value to them. That is, caretakers hope others see the value in their giving nature. They similarly hope the other person they direct their caretaking towards will love them in return. But this never happens in a lasting way. I believe this is due to the fact that caretaking is a <u>unidirectional</u> (one-way) attempt to "exchange" love; caretakers typically get used and eventually rejected or they become worn-out and later blamed for their fatigue and falling short in their relationship responsibilities. Thus, we can see excessive caretaking as the "flight" response in the fight-or-flight reaction our brains produce to perceived threats of harm. It is a "flight" response in regards to people fleeing from expressing their needs to others. In this way they run from themselves and direct their attention to trying to secure love by meeting the needs of others while their own needs are ignored. But, in essence, by caretaking they are actually protecting themselves from feeling the anxieties (this is the "threat") associated with mutual (secure) love relating where both people's needs count and are included into the relationship. If you haven't experienced your needs counting in childhood, or if you have not learned that other people have needs too that must be met in a mutual way, love will always be fleeting for you. That is, unless you make changes in yourself and in how you relate to others. (See Appendix I for a list of 10 Commandments for Caretakers.)

PROBLEM: People get stuck in caretaking and are at a loss about their own needs. Thus, we can see excessive caretaking as the "flight" response in the fight-or-flight reaction our brains produce to perceived threats of harm. It is a "flight" response in regards to people fleeing from expressing their needs to others. In this way they run from themselves and direct their attention to trying to secure love by meeting the needs of others while their own needs are ignored.

SIMPLE SOLUTION 52: Prepare yourself to recalibrate relationships (as well as your nervous systems) towards mutual respect. It takes significant effort to overcome a caretaking polarity, but it is necessary if you seek secure love. (Good thing you're reading this book!)

Selfishness as Fight for Your Needs

Selfishness is the other common reaction to abuse, neglect, or spoiling. It is always an outgrowth of spoiling children and sometimes a reaction to being abused, especially when the abuse occurs through early rejection in life. Perhaps a parent dies early or is unavailable to the child for reasons such as being a single parent, being away at work a lot, or in cases where the child is given up for adoption. In other cases, only-children can be given too much attention without also being taught about the needs of others. Only-children may learn that they are the focus of attention in their families, sometimes by gross negligence of parents' intentional spoiling or at other times inadvertently by simply being the only child or having suffered some type of early childhood illness. Furthermore, spoiling of people can occur in response to their beauty, handsomeness, or special skills. This can be seen in models, celebrities, and athletes. We set people up, both children and adults, by over-admiring them and treating them as if they are extra special. Sometimes people with above average incomes give and buy too much for their children and create selfish people in the process. They watch as their kids struggle to attach securely in a mutual way and try and seduce people to love them because of their financial status, growing ever so frustrated by the lack of security and a sense of feeling used by others. Therefore, there are a variety of ways people learn a selfish way of relating.

However, people who seem to have "selfish-brain disease," a more severe and pervasive form of self-centered relating (narcissism), are more likely to have been abused, neglected, abandoned and/or extensively spoiled. In terms of the fight-or-flight response, selfish people can be viewed as portraying a "fight" for survival. Self-centered people are in a fight for attention. They mistake attention for love. They see their survival, i.e., their need for love, as being obtained only by dominating and gleaning all the attention others have to offer. They battle for love using tools of dominance, personal appeal, sharp dress, physical fitness, special skills, or criticism. Through criticalness, selfish people project their insecurities onto others communicating to them that they are never quite right or acceptable, especially if they decrease the attention they are giving the selfish person and limit the time meeting their needs.

People with selfish brain problems seem to always be saying "look at me" or "take care of me." They typically seek to challenge you or your views, to get you to accept <u>their</u> ways of thinking as your own. Self-centered relating also shows itself when such people show their excessive vulnerabilities through statements like: "I can't do anything right! Or, "I can't live without you (and your undivided attention), and in the extreme, "I will kill myself!" Thus, they dramatically complain of their problems and fight for your attention just as if there was some physical threat to their survival and well-being. They fight for your attention, for they mistakenly think attention is love. This is how their true vulnerabilities and <u>their need for love</u> can be detected; they've got to have your attention or they feel worthless and unloved. They feel very anxious without sufficient attention. But, they will never obtain secure love in this way. Others will be worn out and leave them. Or, narcissists will "fall out of love" with a caretaker, because the natural outcome of selfishness (and caretaking) is a lack of secure attachment and love. Selfish people can travel through life on a search for secure love by going in and out of relationships with caretakers who treat them special for a while, until they too get worn-out, and either leave the selfish person or fail to satisfy their unquenchable thirst for attention. Secure love will never be achieved in this way. (See Appendix II for a list of 10 Commandments for overly "Self-Focused" people.)

PROBLEM: In terms of the fight-or-flight response, selfish people can be viewed as portraying a "fight" for survival. They starve to be the center of attention. They mistake attention for love.

SIMPLE SOLUTION 53: You have to be invested for the long haul if you love a narcissist and want to shape the relationship to a more mutually satisfying one.

People Alternate between Caretaking and Selfishness

People also can alternate between caretaking and selfishness. This is part of what confuses a lot of people, but it is how the human brain seems to be structured. And this is what Mary Jo Fay was referencing in her book about "perfect partners" going bad. Narcissists, and caretakers, can alternate between self-serving and caretaking behaviors even when they are predominantly anchored on one end of the polarity or the other. However, it is out of the feelings of anxiety each feels that cause them to gravitate toward one polarity or the other. There must be communication about mutual needs at the start of any relationship. People also know they must meet the needs of others to initiate time together as through dating. Narcissists can splendidly shower their new partner in love, warmth, and charming transactions. They just can't maintain it because it makes them anxious to do so. Similarly, caretakers can voice some needs and preferences at the start of relationships, but to continue doing so raises their anxieties and they succumb to tending to the needs of others. It is really a disorder of attachment and anxiety that both narcissists <u>and</u> caretakers suffer from. But it seems to be a result of the way the human brain responds to the lack of secure love and attachment or spoiling that result in this pervasive human problem. Humans respond to anxiety and fear associated with the establishment of secure love by fighting for attention or giving out attention in a fight-or-flight fashion.

PROBLEM: People also can alternate between caretaking and selfishness. This is part of what confuses a lot of people, but it is how the human brain seems to be structured. Narcissists can treat another person nice temporarily; they show knowledge of caretaking but can't maintain it.

SIMPLE SOLUTION 54: Try and understand the Polarity of Mind Reflex and the underlying fear narcissists have when it comes to intimacy. They may hate to feel vulnerable, but they will always remain insecure until they learn the skill of mutual relating. Basically, you have to be smarter than your fight-or-flight response to succeed in love!

Chapter 12

TALK THIS WAY TO THE NARCISSIST

Speak Up Language Matters: Changing Fight-or-Flight Language

Caretakers must learn to identify and assert their needs in order to level the playing field with narcissists. Without the ability to identify and voice needs, caretakers don't stand a chance when trying to establish a more secure relationship with a narcissist. That is why the beginning of this book focused on tools to use in identifying needs and voicing them, e.g., FENTECC. However, voicing needs is necessary but not sufficient when trying to establish secure love, especially with a narcissist. Narcissists' fight-or-flight responses react adversely to assertiveness alone.

Language matters. That is, there are ways to use language to get narcissists to consider the needs of others. The ideas I present here make use of the fact that everyone needs love. Furthermore, you must remember that in spite of their show of dominance, specialness, and importance narcissists are very vulnerable and fearful people on the inside. There are ways to use language to help limit the triggering of defensive posturing from narcissists. Words of mutualness are more likely to succeed when conversing with them. Words like "we," "our," and "us." But first, let's talk about the value of the word "no."

The Value of "No"

"Just say no," was Nancy Reagan's mantra in the 80's when husband Ronald was president. "Just say no to drugs," was her advice. It was such a simple statement. Even though she oversimplified drug abuse treatment and the variety of challenges addicts face, being able to say "no" is a vital relationship tool.

I've read many self-help books. I remember reading in one of them how having friends who are able to tell you "no" sometimes is a true example of a healthy and secure relationship. If both parties are able to say "no" when they have to, i.e., if the act of setting limits is acceptable for both parties, then it is a sign of a healthy relationship. People have varying needs and circumstances. This is a fact of life. People have to be able to tell each other "no" sometimes. But both parties should have this right. Again, the mutual respect of needs is the key.

Now, back to our discussion about relationships with narcissists. Telling them "no" can trigger an emotional tantrum tantamount to World War III. Their bid to control their relationship with you is paramount. Once challenged, narcissists reflexively launch an attack. They will attack your thinking, personality, intentions, judgment, or credibility. What they are trying to get from you is a defensive response. If you defend yourself by explaining your views, needs, etc. "they've got ya!" Narcissists are very vulnerable people, but are the last to see this. They need to control you and be above you in status, power, and ideology. Unless they are able to dominate you they are vulnerable to being intimate and close. If you defend yourself to a narcissist they will, of course, question your ideas more. Defending your position to a narcissist allows them to play you like a fish. After all, they don't care what you have to say. They show no listening skill or interest in your ideas and needs. What do they get out of "discussions" structured to question others' judgment but never their own? They get a sense of power and control. Why do they need to control you? So vulnerable they are; defending yourself to them is their way of keeping you at bay and inferior to them. A reasonable and guiding principal for avoiding such conversations is: never remain very long in a conversation with someone who doesn't care what you have to say.

PROBLEM: People stuck in a selfish polarity are extremely bad listeners. After all, listening to another person raises their anxiety because it triggers a loss of attention from themselves and essentially a loss of "love."

SIMPLE SOLUTION 55: Never remain very long in a conversation with someone who doesn't care what you have to say. Simply stop and say, "no" then state a need and walk away for a while. Don't reinforce the other's act of not listening to you by remaining in "conversation" with them.

A comment about assertiveness is warranted here. Similar to saying "no," assertive comments by themselves will trigger a me-versus-you response from a narcissist. They have learned along their road of life that needs have not been reciprocal. And if you only assert your needs they will react similarly to how they respond to the word "no." Yes, being able to act assertively is a critical life skill. But, in dealing with narcissists it is a necessary but insufficient skill with regards to building a mutually respectful relationship. Anything that triggers their me-versus-you thinking (and their fight-or-flight response) is failure ridden for those people wanting to relate to a narcissist.

In review, since narcissists try and set up "conversations" in a me-versus-you style, no matter what you say to them, no matter how factual and reasonable your opinions are, they are unable to accept any opinion that is different from their own. Thus, you must introduce the word "no" in your conversations with narcissists quickly, in response to their criticism (which mostly begins by their use of the word "you") and then make an assertive statement about your needs. However, before stating your need to them, you need to use "bridging" words to lead them toward a mutually respectful structure in relating. This is where words like "we," "our," and "us" come in to play. We will discuss the use of such words in a little bit.

PROBLEM: Guiding narcissists toward mutual relating takes novel skills, attitudes, and perseverance.

SIMPLE SOLUTION 56: You must introduce the word "no" in your conversations with narcissists and introduce it quickly when they start to criticize you. But, before making assertive statements about your needs use "bridging" words to lead them toward a mutually respectful structure in relating. This is where words like "we," "our," and "us" come in to play.

SIMPLE SOLUTION 56 SPECIAL SUPPLEMENT: Here's a "magic" formula to use when you are starting to be criticized by a narcissist. Usually, their criticisms will start with the word "YOU....." and include blame and accusations. Don't delay, however, as soon as you hear the word "YOU" interrupt them and follow the 4 steps/comments below:

1. *Tell them, "No."*

2. *Then say, "We have to respect each other's opinions and needs" (or any other mutual need you want to request.)*

3. *Then say, "I need you to.............." (Pause to assess if they are listening to you).*

4. *And then ask, "What do you need from me?"*

(Repeat the above 4 steps as needed, for example, whenever blame and criticism arises.)

Avoid the Trappings of "Me-Versus-You"

Now is the time to change your focus and conversation with the narcissist. You want to avoid the trappings of a "me-versus-you" dialogue. You have to learn to resist the pull or challenge to directly defend yourself with them. You can still respond to them, but you have to use words that seek to unite rather than divide. Thus, you must follow your use of the word "no" or assertiveness with terms of mutualness. Collaboration, team work, and joining are your new goals, if you decide you want or have to relate to a narcissist. Your choice of words that you use to negotiate with them must "feel good" to their well-established fight-or-flight habits of relating.

The "Chi of <u>We</u>," "The Strength of <u>Our</u>," and, "The Gift of <u>Us</u>"

Let's start with use of the word "we." After a selfish person challenges you, verbally attacks you, blatantly puts you down, or simply tells you how stupid you are for not thinking like them, just tell them "no" (just like Nancy Reagan said). Your dialogue might look like this:

Narcissist: "How stupid are you?"
       Or, "How can you think like that!"

Mutual Attempt: "No, <u>we</u> both have valid points."
       Or, "No, <u>we</u> both have something to offer here."

In contrast, if you were to respond with an "I" statement like: "I disagree….." and then explain yourself, or by telling them, "I need you to listen to me," you will be triggering in their mind a "me-versus-you" reaction. Whenever your language supports such a polarity (me-versus-you) in their minds, psychological defenses are triggered in the narcissist.

Not much good will follow this type of dialogue. You must expose them to words that offer joining not words of division. Another way to think about communications with narcissists is that your language must offer "additive" valuing of needs and not "divisive" or "subtracting." It's like what Winnie the Pooh tells Christopher Robin in *The Hunt for Christopher Robin*: It is his favorite time of day; the time when, "you and me become we." And this is what you want to try to create with the narcissist; mutual respect of needs is the only way for them to establish secure love regardless of whether "they believe" they have such a need for love or not. Narcissists will never get their need for lasting and secure love met by taking, dominating, and not learning to respect others' needs.

PROBLEM: If you plan to "tell-off" a narcissist or only tell them your needs, without interest in theirs' you will meet more resistance and fail to engage them.

SIMPLE SOLUTION 57: Another way to think about communications with narcissists is that your language must offer "additive" valuing of needs--not "divisive" or "subtracting" words.

My main point here is to learn to use language to your advantage. And, understand the Polarity of Mind Reflex and learn to work with it. Yes, you must know how to identify and assert your needs but that is only a stage in development when working toward secure love and attachment. It is not the end point. Your goal is mutualness. The strategic use of language is offered here as a means of building relationships with selfish/narcissistic types.

There is strength in the word "our" as well. For example, after a narcissist criticizes you and after you tell them "no" you might say to them: "Both of our needs must count." Or, "Both of our ideas have merit."

"Our" can also be used in other ways, after the word "no" for example. You might say to a selfish person: "Our marriage can be better than this." Or, "Our relationship can include both our points of view." Also, "Our gain in respect for each other is your gain too." Thus, the word "our" offers an opportunity for additional joining and a tool for shaping mutual respect.

The word "us" can also be used to support mutualness. After saying "no" to a narcissist's criticism, you might say the following: "It is not good for us to fight like this." Or, "What about us both counting?" The use of the word "us" will fit into some conversations and not others. In contrast, words like "we" and "our" are likely to be more easily applied. It is just a matter of language choice; some words are easier to use than others. See what works best for you. Just remember the sequence of wording is important, e.g., use "no" first, followed by statements including "we," "us," and "our," and persevere as you work toward the goal of mutual relating.

One Step Forward, Two Steps Back

The path toward change for narcissists and caretakers has many starts and stops to it. That is, using the tools and knowledge in this book, people often start to see changes in selfish people towards considering other's needs but then "the old self" returns. People sometimes report, "He did a complete turnaround; he became nasty again!" Similarly caretakers report, "Well I did it again, I didn't speak up and state my needs. Why do I do that!" Change is not easy or straight forward for most people polarized in a selfish or caretaking pattern. Feelings of confusion, anxiety, and irritability are frequently associated with important personal growth and development. It seems that "brain change" comes with certain emotional challenges. It is as if your brain recognizes a change related to interpersonal habits of survival is being requested of it. That is, uncomfortable feelings may simply be your brain's feedback to you as to whether you really want to update your survival network or not. Once polarized in a selfish or caretaking fashion it takes time, effort, and perseverance to recalibrate brain patterns for good! You can't see the soupy mixture of chemicals and nerves in your brain that must recalibrate themselves according to your attempts to accomplish mutually respectful habits of relating. Your brain "may think" you are heading in a (previously) unhelpful direction with your needs. That is why the more you can identify and recognize even small changes within yourself and others, the more likely you will be to continue on a course toward establishing secure and lasting love. Fortunately, small changes that bring even small results can feel good and help keep you on track.

Problem: People often feel confused, anxious, or irritable when they start changing long-standing patterns of relating, as they seek mutual respect in relationships.

Simple Solution 58: You must persevere. Consider your uncomfortable feelings as signs that your brain is undergoing major changes in terms of how you get your needs met in relationships. Mutual relating comes with a price—anxiety at first. But don't give up. Such feelings will fade as you experience moments of success!

Other Terms of Endearment and Mutual Relating

Sometimes it helps to point out to a narcissist the things neither one of you wants. For example, neither party wants to be a "victim." Here is a way of introducing this fact to a narcissist and a list of words that describe what each party is trying to avoid. You might point out to a "self-preserving" individual any of the following: "Neither one of us wants to be a: Pawn, Dummy, Minion, Patsy, Servant, Lapdog, Lackey, Flunkey, String-Puppet, Mannequin, Sucker, Fatality, or Casualty." Other terms can also be used to state what you are trying to avoid. For example, "Neither one of us wants to be: Preyed Upon, Duped, Victimized, Neglected, Abused, Rejected, Disregarded, or Devalued." In these examples your dialogue with the narcissist takes on the framework of mutualness. You both want and don't want the same things. Neither of you wants to be victimized or dominated. Words like "we," "us," and "our" serve the purpose of structuring your relationship and dialogue along these lines. The goal of mutual value and relating is fostered in these ways.

PROBLEM: You both want and don't want the same thing: both of you want to be valued and neither of you wants to be victimized or dominated.

SIMPLE SOLUTION 59: Develop your ability to use mutual language.

"Teamwork" has to be emphasized to narcissists. This term can be useful, as narcissists are typically very competitive in nature. Here are related terms to use with narcissists that support a sense of teamwork. "We have to learn to: Compromise, Take Turns, Share Tasks, Give Equal Effort, Cooperate, Make Exchanges, and Share a Game Plan." All these terms can be used to decrease the defensive stance of selfishness (and caretaking).

PROBLEM: Narcissists have been overindulged and spoiled at some point in their lives. No one has required them to take turns and share collaboratively with others.

SIMPLE SOLUTION 60: "Teamwork" has to be emphasized with narcissists. Practice trading needs on a one-to-one basis. For example, one person voices a need and the other person commits to meet it. Immediately afterwards, the other person voices a need and the first person works to meet it. Thus, practice trading needs on a 1:1 ratio when starting the change process with highly polarized people.

The truth is nobody wants to be victimized. We all have to survive. And we all need secure love.

Chapter 13

IN SUMMARY

We have covered a lot of ground in this book. We have explored what happens when fear and related anxieties are imparted to people in their childhoods through abuse, neglect, abandonment and spoiling. We have defined differences in patterns of relating when a person experiences fear or love early on in life. A pyramid for healthy relationships was presented, emphasizing the need for mutual respect in relationships. Again, we discussed how it is only through the mutual respect of needs that secure love can be established and people can trust each other. We learned of the importance of defining needs and were introduced to a tool for doing so called FENTECC. The importance of conflict was explored and a model for mutual solutions to problems was offered. Several conflict tools were presented. Each conflict tool is designed to help navigate some of the tricky and demanding ways people try to exert control over others. In addition, each conflict tool is hoped to be used in a responsible way toward establishing mutual respect across relationships. The importance of feelings was discussed. Emphasis was placed on the nature and origins of feelings and the need to not blame others for all that you feel.

Special attention was given to people suffering from "Selfish-Brain Disease" and how to interact with them to try and establish mutually respectful relating. Much patience and persistence is needed with such people. They are very fearful and anxiety ridden, but often are the last to realize or see it. Specific ways of talking with selfish people were emphasized, especially for those people wanting to try to strengthen mutual ways of relating with them.

And finally, more in-depth discussion was given to the Polarity of Mind Reflex. This phenomenon will hopefully help others to understand the ways in which the brain seeks to reconcile effects of abuse, neglect, abandonment and spoiling. The problems many people have interpersonally can be understood through the Polarity of Mind Reflex as can potential solutions to relationship difficulties arising from it which were explored throughout this book.

In summary then, perhaps there are no good or bad guys here. People need love, but if abused, neglected, abandoned, or spoiled they lose or never learn the ability to be mutually respectful. Thus, narcissism and excessive caretaking are seen as two sides of the same coin. Both represent compromised solutions to achieving secure love relationships. Each is inspired through feelings of insecurity and anxiety felt when engaging in love and other important relationships. Each can be seen as having "selfish" qualities. Narcissists mistake love for attention and want to grab all they can. Caretakers want to give exclusively, never really relying on others to meet their needs. Each "selfishly" seeks to feel good by taking attention or giving it. But, both are doomed to only feel good temporarily. Neither ever establishes secure and lasting love. Each is likely to suffer undo heartaches and headaches as they live out lives marked by fleeting love relationships. You see, you can love someone but never achieve secure attachment unless mutual patterns of relating are established. Without mutual respect of needs in relationships you will always be vulnerable to excessive love losses in life.

The information and guidance offered in this book has been an attempt to bridge the gap between what has previously been overlooked in regards to human relationships and love. We have to get our act together now; mutual respect must be your goal in all relationships. This book includes ways to work towards establishing mutual respect in your lives. Similarly, people have to learn ways to cope with and manage their fears, labeled here as anxieties, in order to ever achieve secure and lasting love. Although not always easy to implement, the suggestions, ideas, and tools in this book can offer you a chance at establishing mutually respectful relationships in your life and the lasting love that goes with it. I wish you the best of luck in transforming your relationships into mutually respectful ones and gaining the security and health that secure love offers. (A few additional tips for fostering attachment are included in Appendix III: Fundamental Attachment Behaviors.)

And finally, some closing words and advice by the Dumbledore character from the Harry Potter movie Deathly Hallows Part Two. Dumbledore is talking to Harry in a scene suggestive of a heaven-like setting. In trying to reassure Harry he says: "Words are in my not so humble opinion our most inexhaustible source of magic, capable of both inflicting injury and remedying it…do not pity the dead Harry, pity the living and above all (pity) those who live without (secure) love."

The End

APPENDIX 1

10 COMMANDMENTS
FOR CARETAKERS

1. Thou shalt always seek the mutual respect of needs; both people's needs must count if secure love is your goal. And that includes your needs too.

2. Thou shalt first learn to identify and speak of your needs. This can be hard for you, but you must keep at it.

3. Thou shalt be as specific with your needs as possible.

4. Thou shalt not refer to the fact that you have needs as "selfish."

5. Thou shalt ask what the other person's needs are after first voicing your own needs to them.

6. Thou shalt pay attention to your true feelings and not deny them. That is, don't tell yourself "not to feel the way you do." Accept what you feel. Then define your needs.

7. Thou shalt translate feelings into needs, and work to state your needs first, before saying anything about your feelings as much as possible.

8. Thou shalt realize that you will likely have to talk about the times in your past when others blatantly dismissed your needs, such as during childhood or in other important relationships.

This will help you to erase roadblocks getting in the way of expressing your needs now. Psychotherapy and counseling can help you do this.

9. Thou shalt not mistakenly assume that all you feel currently is being caused by other people today, especially if you have been abused or neglected by others in the past. Thus, do not blame others for your feelings but work to make your needs known now.

10. Thou shalt learn that compromising does not mean giving in totally to the needs of others. You must voice your needs no matter how small they are.

APPENDIX II

10 COMMANDMENTS FOR HIGHLY SELF-PRESERVING PEOPLE

1. Thou shalt always seek the mutual respect of needs. Both people's needs must count if secure love is your goal. Learn to ask others what they need daily. You should realize that you'll have to allow others' needs to count first at the start of conversations. But your needs will get to count too. Learn to take turns.

2. Thou shalt realize that you need secure and lasting love too. You may unfortunately only realize this when your partner decides to leave you. You will have to learn to say you are sorry and also how to repair relationships where your needs have dominated.

3. Thou shalt not misperceive love as being the same thing as attention. Love is only securely established when you work to value the other person's needs and not just your own. Remember, neither one of you wants to be a victim.

4. Thou shalt be kind to yourself and acknowledge your confusion or fears about needing secure and lasting love. Do not blame the other person for how you feel. Do not tell the other person they are "selfish" or "crazy" when they tell you their needs or what it has been like for them to be in a relationship with you.

5. Thou shalt fight the impulse to dominate others by focusing too much on your ideas and talents. Take turns. Stop and ask others about their ideas and needs. Listen to them. Keep your words

and promises. Remember, each of you wants to be listened to. Both of you get to count, that is if your goal is to construct secure lasting relationships.

6. Thou shalt realize that you will need to talk about the experiences in your past that taught you either that your needs did not count or that your needs counted exclusively and at the expense of others. For example, being spoiled may feel good temporarily as a child, but it interferes with the ability to have a mutually respectful relationship later on. The sooner this is realized, the better. Learn how to share attention and gain secure love.

7. Thou shalt work on seeing and understanding the needs of others. Prove to others that you are listening to them by summarizing what they are telling you, even if you don't agree with them. It is OK to ask others to take turns and listen to you too. But don't forget the "take turns" part. It is your life line to secure relationships.

8. Thou shalt encourage mutual forms of relating with others, to protect yourself from being victimized and to help protect you from losses incurred by victimizing others. Use the word "we" as much as possible in your conversations with others. Try it, you'll like it!

9. Thou shalt learn to translate your feelings into specific needs as your main tool towards decreasing anxiety about mutual needs management. Make your needs known directly, but not through criticism or complaints. Don't half communicate with people. Don't expect people to "read your mind" and finish your thoughts or sentences for you. Learn to have courage and state your needs yourself. Then, continue to show interest in the other's needs, back-and-forth, with give and take and compromises.

10. Thou shalt learn to manage your anxiety and irritations about exchanging needs with others. Remember, you can get what you need in relationships but not through patterns that are unidirectional and only self-serving in nature. You won't be abandoned and you won't fall out of love if the mutual exchange of needs is incorporated into your relationships.

APPENDIX III

FUNDAMENTAL ATTACHMENT BEHAVIORS

1. SPEND TIME TOGETHER

2. MAINTAIN EYE CONTACT

3. TALK TO EACH OTHER

4. LISTEN TO EACH OTHER (PEOPLE FEEL SAFER WHEN YOU <u>SHOW</u> UNDERSTANDING). SUMMARIZE TO THE OTHER PERSON WHAT YOU HEAR THEM SAYING, EVEN IF YOU HAVE TO SIMPLY REPEAT THEIR WORDS BACK TO THEM.

5. TELL PERSON YOUR NEEDS

6. CARE ABOUT THE OTHER PERSON'S NEEDS TOO

7. SHARE POSITIVE FEELINGS AND TERMS OF ENDEARMENT, E.G., "I LIKE YOU!" AND SMILE AT EACH OTHER

8. LAUGH WITH EACH OTHER; SHARE HUMOR

9. TOUCH EACH OTHER; SHOW PHYSICAL AFFECTION

10. BE ACCOUNTABLE AND A PERSON WHO KEEPS THEIR PROMISES

APPENDIX IV

JOURNALING AS AN AID FOR IDENTIFYING YOUR NEEDS (AND MEETING YOUR NEXT BEST FRIEND)

Journaling can be like having a best friend. That is, a best friend who is available day or night to give you feedback about your life problems, feelings, and related needs. If you have a history of engaging in excessive caretaking, close friends may be hard for you to come by at times of trouble. That's because friendships need to be mutual in nature to be lasting and reliable. Caretaking, by itself, does not necessarily produce friendships you can count on. You must ask to have your needs met in relationships in order to have secure attachments with others. But journaling is available to you anytime and anywhere. Journaling is also private; like a good friend who can keep your thoughts and concerns confidential. Furthermore, the process of journaling and the act of learning to get your needs met can lead you closer to establishing enduring relationships with others. Thus, as you learn to journal in ways described below and do it on a daily basis a transformation can occur in your life that can have far reaching effects. Journaling can help lead you to greater happiness, more life satisfaction, and the establishment of lasting love relationships. And it is free!

Additional Benefits of Journaling

One of the most challenging aspects of journaling (and perhaps your life), in addition to identifying your needs, is the challenge to lessen the amount of denial you have engaged in regarding your true feelings and personal history. This is especially true for caretakers. Caretakers get into the habit of both meeting the needs of others and, if they have a need, projecting their needs onto other people through heightened empathy and sympathy. There is simply too much indirect need seeking going on with caretakers along with an over use of denial regarding the fact they have any needs at all. That is, if you don't know your needs you are very likely denying your true feelings. And if you deny how you really feel you are out of alignment with yourself. Remember, your feelings are feedback from your brain about the state of your being, including both your physical and emotional health needs. Thus, if you are out of touch and misalignment with yourself you are less likely to be healthy (or happy).

A notebook and pen (or personal computer) can be used to help create many more life opportunities than you ever imagined. This will be particularly true if you use your journal time to identify your actual unfiltered feelings and your needs related to them. In addition, journaling can be used to replace your reliance on other substances like food and alcohol or other compulsive behaviors that may already be having negative effects on your health. Thus, journaling serves as a replacement tool for less healthy methods of coping with life stress.

Furthermore, journaling helps people identify specific goals to work on that might get overlooked when treatment only focuses on surface issues such as binge eating, alcohol abuse, or other compulsive acts. Such problems or goals can be critical to lessening a person's use of substances for emotional reasons. An individual's problems may include marital or family problems, underlying problems with depression, worry, or anxiety, unresolved histories of child abuse, negative effects from other abusive relationships, and problems related to body image or self-esteem. Journaling in ways described here can be a starting point to changing these and other underlying problems that previously supported substance abuses.

Journaling can also help you make better use of your time if you are participating in mental health counseling services with a licensed professional. You can start your sessions, say for example on a weekly basis, having worked on yourself and identifying the goals and needs of most relevance to you. You and your therapist might both appreciate and benefit by your journaling between sessions.

Journal Outline

PART ONE

We will refer to the journal as S&W or "Stress and Wishes" journal. The journal is divided into 3 parts. <u>The first part involves writing about the stressors you experience each day.</u> Stressors include <u>any</u> problems, difficulties, irritations, or annoyances that make you mad, worried, or even a little bit annoyed. When you start your journal entry, it might help you to imagine yourself talking to a friend who you know will keep things private between the two of you. Just freely tell them your stories about your day (by writing about them). Most people go through a stage of minimizing daily stressors and it quickly becomes evident because they don't know what to write about. For example, some people start off with believing "if you don't see a problem or acknowledge one then it doesn't exist," right? They may quickly give-up journaling and resist it at first. Remember, many people, especially those diligently living out the role of caretaker, are doing battle with an omnipotent foe: denial. This coping habit is tougher to overcome than many people realize. Thus, don't be discouraged if you can't think of what to write about at first. Keep trying and stop ignoring what your heart is telling you about what you actually feel. Just write about what concerns you without criticalness or self-judgment.

Some people need help identifying their daily stressors. You might want to ask yourself, "Now what kinds of things bothered me today?" Try and not filter or edit anything that comes to your mind that was, perhaps, even only a slight irritant. Furthermore, the relationship between current stressors and past experiences (your childhood or experiences in other significant relationships) often needs consideration but you have to think openly without self-judgment to let such important reflections from your past appear. Again, try not to filter or minimize your thoughts and memories from your past. Eventually, as journaling continues, the relationship of current day stressors to issues from your past grows and becomes more evident. The challenge is to keep working at the journal long enough to lessen denial, increase self-awareness, see the relationship stressors have to unhealthy or compulsive behaviors, and start to work at other solutions to problems. Perseverance is necessary. Don't let denial defeat you.

PART TWO

<u>The second part of the S&W journal includes writing about your wishes, wants and needs.</u> However, this part of the journal is not actually about "wishes," but more about specific wants and needs related to your problems and thus your feelings. But, at least to start with, my experience has taught me that it is easier for people to consider what they "wish" could be different and later their "wants and needs." A "wish" can be viewed as a successive approximation to lessening denial about solutions to your problems. It also serves as a transition towards greater assertiveness and self-worth that corresponds to identifying and asserting your wants and needs. This, I believe, is the "silver-tuna" goal when treating emotional eating in particular. Becoming assertive about specific wants and needs is critical for overcoming denial's toxic effects and increasing self-worth. It also supports the reduction of victimization so often experienced by emotional eaters.

Another important issue that needs to be addressed that typically arises through journaling, is why substances like food, alcohol, or other compulsive behaviors have become so important as a means of coping with life stress. In comparison and more pointedly, why aren't people more included in your support network? Ultimately, the personal issues that interfere with you accessing other people for comfort and support need to be modified. This is another major role for licensed mental health professionals, when you consult with them. It is hard to replace food, or other addictive substances, if the barriers interfering with interpersonal attachment are not lessened. And lessened they must be; people must learn how to get their needs met through relationships with other people. Learning to identify your daily stressors, any associations they have towards previous life experiences that were perhaps traumatic, and specifying the needs you continue to have related to them must all be part of your journaling and related life enhancement. Thereafter, courage is required as you start to voice and assert your needs and work towards building more mutually respectful relationships.

PART THREE

The third part of the S&W journal is to define the action steps you will take to meet your needs. After a person goes through the efforts of identifying stressors and defining needs they must define for themselves what action steps they are going to take and when. For example, a person must decide who they will make their needs known to and exactly what they will say. They also must define a time, day, or a situation when they will put the action into effect. Action steps can take the most effort for people to accomplish. But like most good things in life, with great effort come progress and the most rewards. Persevere you must. Never give up seeking to get your needs met. Seek mutual respect of needs across all relationships, and enjoy the benefits of a more fulfilling and loving life!

RECOMMENDED READING LIST

Bandler, R. & Grinder, J. 1976. *The Structure of Magic. Palo Alto, CA:* Science and Behavior Books

Barshinger, C.E., Larowe, L.E., & Tapia, A.T. 1995. *Haunted Marriage: Overcoming the Ghosts our Your Spouse's Childhood Abuse.* Madison, WI: InterVarsity Press

Behary,W.T. 2008. *Disarming the Narcissist: Surviving and Surviving with the Self-Absorbed.* Oakland, CA: New Harbinger Publications, Inc.

Bettelheim, B. 1950. *Love is Not Enough.* New York: The Free Press

Braiker, H.B. 2001. *The Disease to Please.* New York: McGraw-Hill Publications

Brown, N. 2002. *Working with the Self-Absorbed.* Oakland, CA: New Harbinger Publications, Inc.

Brown, N. 2001. *Children of the Self-Absorbed.* Oakland, CA: New Harbinger Publications, Inc.

Calkins, S.D. & Hill, A. 2007. Caregiver Influences on emerging emotion regulation. Biological and environmental transactions in early development. In J.J. Gross (Ed.) *Handbook of Emotion Regulation.* NewYork: Guilford Press. (Cited by Beischel, M. Ed.D. 2010. Workshop : Attachment and Emotional regulation.)

Cavaiola, A.A. 2000. *Toxic Coworkers: How to deal with Dysfunctional People on the Job.* Oakland, CA: New Harbinger Publications, Inc.

Cloud, H. & Townsend, J. 1995. *Safe People.* Grand Rapids, MI: Zondervan.

Fay, M.J. 2008. *When Your Perfect Partner Goes Perfectly Wrong.* Parker, Colorado: Out of the Box Inc.

Hanson, R. & Mendius, R, *Buddha's Brain.* Oakland, California: New Harbinger Publications, Inc.

Lerner, R. 2009. *The Object of my Affection is in my Reflection: Coping with Narcissists.* Deerfield Beach, FL: Health Communications, Inc.

Lucas, M. 2012. *Rewire Your Brain For Love, U.S.A.: Hay House, Inc.*

Payson, E. D. 2002. *The Wizard of Oz and Other Narcissists; Coping with the One-Way Relationship in Work, Love, and Family.* Royal Oak, MI: Julian Day Publications.

Pelletier, K.R. 1977. *Mind as Healer, Mind as Slayer.* New York: Dell Publishing

Seligmen, M. 2007. *The Optimistic Child.* New York: Houghton Mifflin Company

Siegel, B.S. 1990. *Peace, Love, & Healing.* New York: Harper & Row

Silverstein, S. 1964. *The Giving Tree.* New York: Harper & Row

Vaknin, S. 1999. *Malignant Self Love: Narcissism Revisited.* Republic of Macedonia: Copyright Lidija Rangelouska

Yudofsky, S.C. 2005. *Fatal Flaws: Navigating Destructive Relationships with People with Disorders of Personality and Character.* Arlington, VA: American Psychiatric Publishing, Inc.

INDEX

Italic page numbers refer to diagrams.

Index created by:

Allegheny Writing &
Publishing Services, L.L.C.
www.awps.biz ~ indexer@awps.biz

29083259R00102

Made in the USA
Middletown, DE
06 February 2016